MobX Quick Start Guide

Supercharge the client state in your React apps with MobX

Pavan Podila
Michel Weststrate

BIRMINGHAM - MUMBAI

MobX Quick Start Guide

Commissioning Editor: Kunal Chaudari
Acquisition Editor: Reshma Raman
Content Development Editor: Aditi Gour
Technical Editor: Sushmeeta Jena
Copy Editor: Safis Editing
Project Coordinator: Hardik Bhinde
Proofreader: Safis Editing
Indexer: Aishwarya Gangawane
Graphics: Jason Monteiro
Production Coordinator: Arvindkumar Gupta

First published: July 2018

Production reference: 1230718

Published by Packt Publishing Ltd.
Livery Place
35 Livery Street
Birmingham
B3 2PB, UK.

ISBN 978-1-78934-483-7

www.packtpub.com

To my loving wife, Sirisha Vardhani, for supporting me all along.

– Pavan Podila

To my kids, Noa and Veria, who have to regularly pull me back to Earth when my thoughts are wandering off. To my wife, Elise, who always encourages me to pursue new ideas. To God, who shared His ability to be a creator with all of us.

– Michel Weststrate

`mapt.io`

Mapt is an online digital library that gives you full access to over 5,000 books and videos, as well as industry leading tools to help you plan your personal development and advance your career. For more information, please visit our website.

Why subscribe?

- Spend less time learning and more time coding with practical eBooks and Videos from over 4,000 industry professionals

- Improve your learning with Skill Plans built especially for you

- Get a free eBook or video every month

- Mapt is fully searchable

- Copy and paste, print, and bookmark content

PacktPub.com

Did you know that Packt offers eBook versions of every book published, with PDF and ePub files available? You can upgrade to the eBook version at `www.PacktPub.com` and as a print book customer, you are entitled to a discount on the eBook copy. Get in touch with us at `service@packtpub.com` for more details.

At `www.PacktPub.com`, you can also read a collection of free technical articles, sign up for a range of free newsletters, and receive exclusive discounts and offers on Packt books and eBooks.

Foreword

I started my journey on Reactive Programming several years ago, when Reactive Programming on frontend wasn't "a thing".

At the beginning, there weren't many references or books available to apply this paradigm on frontend applications; therefore, I had to spent a lot of time extracting the key concepts of Reactive Programming from books on Java or Clojure, university white papers, and blog posts.

In the past two years though, slowly but steadily, the community started developing many frameworks and libraries that shape the frontend Reactive ecosystem we know nowadays.

Reactive Programming is getting a lot of traction. Companies such as Netflix, Microsoft, IBM, and many others are using this paradigm, leveraging the strong decoupling provided out of the box by this paradigm and the unidirectional data flow used in many Reactive state management systems.

From the developers, community, we had a strong push on sharing great reactive implementations, such as Rx.JS, Cycle.js, VueX, SAM patterns, Angular with NGRX, and many others.

There is one though that is standing out from the crowd, created by a bunch of smart developers; it is called *MobX*.

MobX is the perfect companion for starting your journey on Reactive Programming. It is easy to learn, applies reactivity with a few lines of code, and it could be used without deeply knowing this paradigm. It can also be used for digging into the reactive programming roots.

MobX ecosystem provides the flexibility of structuring small projects, such as a **Proof of Concept (PoC)**, or large projects managed by several teams, thanks to **MobX State Tree (MST)**.

I had the opportunity to work on both MobX and MST: I created some simple PoCs for validating my theories, and also architected a micro-frontend system with tens of developers working with MST.

I saw how well thought out and designed this system was and how fast it was, picking it up from scratch, by other developers.

As you will discover in these pages, MobX will provide you with the flexibility smartness behind architectural and design decisions that you were looking for. It is the perfect companion for any experienced person or a newcomer to the reactive programming movement.

Enjoy your journey into MobX and MST, I'm sure you won't regret it!

Luca Mezzalira

Author, Speaker, Chief Architect at DAZN, Google Developer Expert and manager of the London JavaScript community

Contributors

About the authors

Pavan Podila has been building frontend applications since 2001 and has used a variety of tools, technologies, and platforms, from Java Swing, WPF with .Net/C#, Cocoa on macOS and iOS, to the web platform with frameworks such as React and Angular. He has been working with React since 2013 and MobX since 2016. He is a colead of the Interactive Practice at *Publicis.Sapient*, where he builds large financial applications for web and mobile platforms.

He has been a Microsoft MVP for client application development (2008-2011), and a published author of *WPF Control Development Unleashed* (Addison-Wesley). He created *QuickLens*, a Mac app for UI designers/developers, and authored several articles and video courses on *Tuts+*.

Pavan is a **Google Developer Expert** (**GDE**) for web technologies and currently authors courses on *The UI Dev*. He is a regular speaker at meetups, conferences, and workshops. When time permits, you can find him sketching on iPad or playing ping-pong.

Michel Weststrate (Msc) is tech lead and open source evangelist at Mendix. He has been active as both a frontend and backend developer in different stacks. An occasional speaker at software conferences, he has authored video courses on egghead.

Intrigued by several (transparent) reactive programming libraries, he researched and worked on making the ReactJS framework more reactive while addressing predictability and maintainability constraints in other solutions. This led to mobservable (nowadays *MobX*), which was quickly adopted at Mendix.

He's very active in the open source software community, and he authored MobX, Immer, and several small libraries, and coauthored MST.

About the reviewer

Naresh Bhatia is a passionate technologist and architect who has spent his career helping developers write better software. He leads the Visualization Practice at *Publicis.Sapient*, which builds interfaces and data visualizations for financial institutions and energy firms. Before joining Sapient, he founded a startup that built domain modeling, code generation, and reverse engineering tools. Naresh graduated with a master's degree in electrical engineering from Illinois Institute of Technology.

Packt is searching for authors like you

If you're interested in becoming an author for Packt, please visit `authors.packtpub.com` and apply today. We have worked with thousands of developers and tech professionals, just like you, to help them share their insight with the global tech community. You can make a general application, apply for a specific hot topic that we are recruiting an author for, or submit your own idea.

Table of Contents

Preface

Reactive programming has captured the imagination of programmers for decades. Once the gang of four standardized the **observer** design pattern, the term has become part of the standard vocabulary of every programmer:

> **Observer** : *Define a one-to-many dependency between objects so that when one object changes state, all its dependents are notified and updated automatically.*

> – *Design Patterns, Erich Gamma, Richard Helm, Ralph Johnson, John Vlissides, 1995*

Nonetheless, there is a wide variety of technologies, libraries, and frameworks implementing the observer pattern. Yet, MobX is unique in the way it applies this pattern to state-management. It has a very friendly syntax, a small core API that makes it easy to learn as a beginner, and it can be applied in any JavaScript project. Moreover, the library has proven scalable, not just at Mendix where the project was first applied, but also in famous projects, such as Microsoft Outlook, Battlefield 1 by DICE, Jenkins, Coinbase, and many, many more.

This book will not just guide you through the basics; it will also immerse you in the philosophy of MobX: *Anything that can be derived from the application state, should be derived. Automatically.*

MobX is not the first of its kind, but it is standing on the shoulders of giants and has pushed the boundaries of what is possible with the transparent reactive programming paradigm. For example, it is, as far as the authors know, the first major library that combines reactivity with synchronous transactions and the first to explicitly distinguish the concept of derived-values and automatic side effects (reactions).

Unlike many learning materials, this book guides you through the inner workings of MobX and its many extension points. This book will hopefully leave a lasting impression that an essentially simple (and very readable!) paradigm can be used to accomplish tasks that are very challenging, not just in terms of **domain complexity**, but also in terms of performance.

Who this book is for

State management plays a crucial role in any application where state is relevant across different places in the code base. This is either because there are multiple consumers or multiple producers of data. In practice, this means that MobX is useful in any application that has a non-trivial amount of data entry or data visualization.

MobX has official bindings for React.js, Preact, and Angular. However, many have used the library in combination with libraries and frameworks such as jQuery, konva.js, Next.js, Vue.js, and even Backbone. When working through the book, you will discover that the concepts required to use a tool like MobX are universally applicable in any environment.

What this book covers

Chapter 1, *Introduction to State Management*, starts with a conceptual treatment of *state-management* and its many nuances. It introduces the side-effect model and prepares you with the philosophy needed to understand MobX. Finally, it gives a speed tour of MobX and some of its core building blocks.

Chapter 2, *Observables, Actions, and Reactions*, takes a deeper look at the core building blocks of MobX. It shows you the various ways of creating observables, using actions to cause mutations on the observables, and, finally, the use of reactions to react to any changes happening on the observables. These three form the core triad of MobX.

Chapter 3, *A React App with MobX*, combines the knowledge gained so far to power a React App with MobX. It tackles the use case of searching books in an online store. The app is built by first identifying the core observable state, using actions to mutate the state, and using reactions via the observer() utility from mobx-react. The React components are the observers that react to changes in the observable state and automatically render the new state. This chapter will give you an early taste of how simple MobX can be for state management in React apps.

Chapter 4, *Crafting the Observable Tree*, puts laser focus on designing the observable state with the various options in MobX. We will tackle how to limit the observability in MobX and learn how to create a tight observable state that only observes the necessary and nothing more. In addition to limiting observability, we will also see how to expand the observability with extendObservable(). Finally, we will look into computed properties and look at the use of ES2015 classes to model the observable state.

Chapter 5, *Derivations, Actions, and Reactions*, goes further into the core building blocks of MobX and explores the API in greater detail. It also touches upon the philosophies governing these building blocks. By the end of this chapter, you will cement your understanding and core intuitions around MobX.

Chapter 6, *Handling Real-World Use Cases*, is where we apply MobX to two important real-world use cases: form handling and page routing. Both are very visual in nature, but we will argue that they can be dealt with much more easily when represented as observable state, actions, and reactions in MobX. This representation makes the React components (the *observers*) a natural visual extension of the state. We will also develop our core intuitions around state modelling with MobX.

Chapter 7, *Special API for Special Cases*, is a survey of APIs that are low level and capable but hide in the shadows of the top-level APIs. such as `observable()`, `action()`, `computed()`, and `reaction()`. We will explore these low-level APIs and then take a brief tour of the debug utilities available for MobX developers. It is comforting to know that MobX has your back from all angles, even in those rare, odd cases.

Chapter 8, *Exploring mobx-utils and mobx-state-tree*, gives you a taste of some useful packages that can simplify the everyday use cases encountered in MobX-driven development. As the name suggests, mobx-utils is a utility tool belt containing an assortment of functions. On the other hand is the powerful mobx-state-tree, commonly referred to as MST, that prescribes an approach for scalable MobX applications, baking in patterns that you get for free, once you adopt the MST style of thinking. It is a worthy upgrade to MobX and a must-have for serious users.

Chapter 9, *MobX Internals*, is where we culminate by peeling off the layers and peeking into the inner workings of MobX. The core abstractions are surprisingly simple and well defined, and they neatly separate the responsibilities. If the term *transparent functional reactive programming* sounds like a black art, this is the chapter that will unravel the magic and reveal how MobX embraces it. This chapter is also an initiation into the MobX code base and a worthy read for anyone aspiring to be a core contributor to the MobX project.

To get the most out of this book

MobX is typically used in programming environments where long-living, in-memory state plays an important role, most notably web, mobile, and desktop applications. The book requires basic understanding of the JavaScript programming language, and will use modern ES2015 syntax in its examples. Frontend examples are based on the ReactJS framework, so some familiarity with it will be useful, but it's not necessary.

Download the example code files

You can download the example code files for this book from your account at www.packtpub.com. If you purchased this book elsewhere, you can visit www.packtpub.com/support and register to have the files emailed directly to you.

You can download the code files by following these steps:

1. Log in or register at www.packtpub.com.
2. Select the **SUPPORT** tab.
3. Click on **Code Downloads & Errata**.
4. Enter the name of the book in the **Search** box and follow the onscreen instructions.

Once the file is downloaded, please make sure that you unzip or extract the folder using the latest version of:

- WinRAR/7-Zip for Windows
- Zipeg/iZip/UnRarX for Mac
- 7-Zip/PeaZip for Linux

The code bundle for the book is also hosted on GitHub at https://github.com/PacktPublishing/MobX-Quick-Start-Guide. In case there's an update to the code, it will be updated on the existing GitHub repository.

We also have other code bundles from our rich catalog of books and videos available at https://github.com/PacktPublishing/. Check them out!

Download the color images

We also provide a PDF file that has color images of the screenshots/diagrams used in this book. You can download it here: http://www.packtpub.com/sites/default/files/downloads/MobXQuickStartGuide_ColorImages.pdf.

Code in Action

Visit the following link to check out videos of the code being run:
http://bit.ly/2NEww85

Conventions used

There are a number of text conventions used throughout this book.

CodeInText: Indicates code words in text, database table names, folder names, filenames, file extensions, pathnames, dummy URLs, user input, and Twitter handles. Here is an example: "Mount the downloaded WebStorm-10*.dmg disk image file as another disk in your system."

A block of code is set as follows:

```
connect(mapStateToProps, mapDispatchToProps, mergeProps,
options)(Component)
```

When we wish to draw your attention to a particular part of a code block, the relevant lines or items are set in bold:

```
import { observable, autorun, action } from 'mobx';

let cart = observable({
    itemCount: 0,
    modified: new Date(),
});
```

Any command-line input or output is written as follows:

```
$ mkdir css
$ cd css
```

Bold: Indicates a new term, an important word, or words that you see onscreen. For example, words in menus or dialog boxes appear in the text like this. Here is an example: "Select **System info** from the **Administration** panel."

Warnings or important notes appear like this.

Tips and tricks appear like this.

Get in touch

Feedback from our readers is always welcome.

General feedback: Email feedback@packtpub.com and mention the book title in the subject of your message. If you have questions about any aspect of this book, please email us at questions@packtpub.com.

Errata: Although we have taken every care to ensure the accuracy of our content, mistakes do happen. If you have found a mistake in this book, we would be grateful if you would report this to us. Please visit www.packtpub.com/submit-errata, selecting your book, clicking on the Errata Submission Form link, and entering the details.

Piracy: If you come across any illegal copies of our works in any form on the Internet, we would be grateful if you would provide us with the location address or website name. Please contact us at copyright@packtpub.com with a link to the material.

If you are interested in becoming an author: If there is a topic that you have expertise in and you are interested in either writing or contributing to a book, please visit authors.packtpub.com.

Reviews

Please leave a review. Once you have read and used this book, why not leave a review on the site that you purchased it from? Potential readers can then see and use your unbiased opinion to make purchase decisions, we at Packt can understand what you think about our products, and our authors can see your feedback on their book. Thank you!

For more information about Packt, please visit packtpub.com.

1
Introduction to State Management

The heart of your React app lives in the client state (data) and is rendered via React components. Managing this state can become tricky as you tackle **user interactions** (UI), perform async operations, and handle domain logic. In this chapter, we will start with a conceptual model of state management in UI, the role of side effects, and the flow of data.

Then, we will take a quick tour of MobX and introduce its core concepts. These concepts will help in drawing some comparisons with Redux. You will see that MobX turns out to be a more *declarative* form of Redux!

The topics covered in this chapter are as follows:

- What is the client state?
- The side effect model
- A speed tour of MobX

The client state

The UI that you can see and manipulate on screen is the result of painting a visual representation of data. The shape of data hints at the kind of controls you provide for visualizing and manipulating this data. For example, if you have a list of items, you will likely show a `List` control that has an array of `ListItems`. Operations may include *searching, paginating, filtering, sorting,* or *grouping* the items in the list. The state of these operations is also captured as data and informs the visual representation.

The following diagram shows the direct relationship of an *array* with a *List* control:

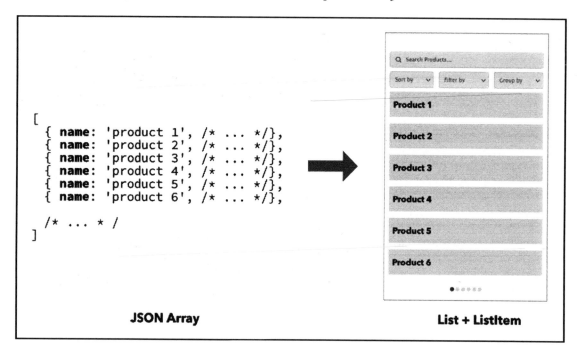

In short, it is the *data* that takes on a pivotal role in describing the UI. Handling the structure and managing the changes that can happen to this data is what we commonly refer to as **state management**. State is just a synonym for the client-data that is rendered on the UI.

 State management is the act of defining the shape of data and the operations that are used to manipulate it. In the context of the UI, it is called *client-side* state management.

As the complexity of the UI increases, more state is accumulated on the client. It gets to a point where state becomes the ultimate source of truth for whatever we see on the screen. This approach to UI development, where we elevate the importance of the client-state, has been one of the biggest shifts in the frontend world. There is an interesting equation that captures this relationship between UI and state:

$$UI = fn(State)$$

`fn` is a transformation function that is applied on the state (the data) that produces a corresponding UI. In fact, a subtle meaning that is hidden here is that, given the same state, `fn` always produces the same UI.

In the context of React, the preceding equation can be written as follows:

$$VirtualDOM = fn(props, state)$$

The only difference here is that `fn` takes two inputs, `props` and `state`, which is the prescribed contract of a React component.

Handling changes in state

However, the preceding equation is only giving half the story of a UI. It's true that the visual representation is derived from the state (through the transformation function, `fn`), but it does not account for the *user operations* that occur on the UI. It's like we have completely ignored the *user* in the equation. After all, the interface is not just used to visually represent data (state), but to also allow the manipulation of that data.

This is where we need to introduce the concept of **actions** that represent these user operations, which results in a change in state. Actions are the commands that you invoke as a result of various input-events that are fired. These actions cause a change in the state, which is then reflected back on the UI.

We can visualize the triad of **State**, **UI**, and **Actions** in the following figure:

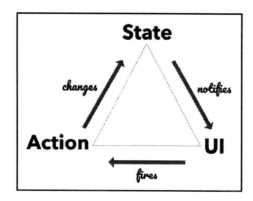

It is worth noting that the UI does not change the state directly, but instead does it via a *message-passing* system by firing *actions*. The *action* encapsulates the parameters that are required to cause the appropriate change in state. The UI is responsible for capturing various kinds of user events (clicks, keyboard presses, touches, voice, and so on) and *translating* them into one or more actions that are then fired to change the state.

When the **State** changes, it notifies all of its observers (subscribers) of the change. The **UI** is also one of the most important subscribers that is notified. When that happens, it re-renders and updates to the new state. This system of data flow from the **State** into the **UI** is always uni-directional and has become the cornerstone of state management in modern UI development.

One of the biggest benefits of this approach is that it becomes easy to grasp how the UI is kept in sync with changing data. It also cleanly separates the responsibilities between *rendering* and *data changes*. The React framework has really embraced this uni-directional data flow and you will see this adopted and extended in **MobX** as well.

The side effect model

Now that we understand the roles of UI, state, and actions, we can extend this to build a mental model of how a UI needs to operate. Reflecting back on the triad of `Action -> State --> UI`, we can make some interesting observations that are not clearly answered. Let's think about how we would handle operations such as the following:

- Downloading data from a server
- Persisting data back on the server

- Running a timer and doing something periodically
- Executing some validation logic when some state changes

These are things that don't fit nicely in our data flow triad. Clearly, we are missing something here, right? You might argue that you could put these operations inside the UI itself and fire actions at certain times. However, that would tack on additional responsibilities to the UI, complicating its operation and also making it difficult to test. From a more academic perspective, it would also violate the **Single Responsibility Principle (SRP)**. SRP states that a class or a module should have only one reason to change. If we start handling additional operations in the UI, it would have more than one reason to change.

So, it seems like we have some opposing forces in action here. We want to retain the purity of the data flow triad, handle ancillary operations such as the ones mentioned in the preceding list, and not add extra responsibilities to the UI. To balance all of these forces, we need to think about the ancillary operations as something *external* to the data flow triad. We call these **side effects**.

Side effects are a result of some state-change and are invoked by responding to the notifications coming from the state. Just like the UI, there is a handler, which we can call the *side effect handler*, that observes (subscribes to) the state change notifications. When a matching state change happens, the corresponding side effect is invoked:

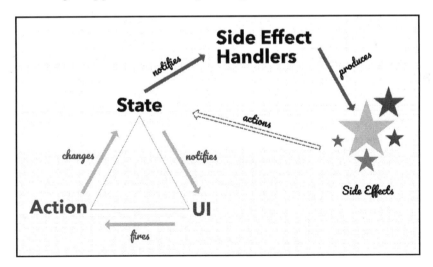

There can be many side effect handlers in the system, and each of them is an observer of the state. When a part of the state they are observing changes, they will invoke the corresponding side effects. Now, these side effects can also cause a change in state by firing additional actions.

As an example, you could fire an action from the UI to download some data. This results in a state change to some flag, which results in notifications being fired to all the observers. A side effect handler that is observing the flag will see the change and trigger a network call to download data. When the download completes, it will fire an action to update the state with the new data.

The fact that *side effects* can also fire actions to update the state is an important detail that helps in completing the loop around managing state. So, it's not just the UI that can cause state changes, but also external operations (via side effects) that can affect a state change. This is the mental model of *side effects*, which can be used to develop your UI and manage the state that it renders. The model is quite powerful and scales very well over time. Later in this chapter and also throughout this book, you will see how MobX makes this *side effect* model a reality and fun to use.

With these concepts in mind, we are now ready to enter the world of MobX.

A speed tour of MobX

MobX is a reactive state management library that makes it easy to adopt the side effect model. Many of the concepts in MobX directly mirror the terminology we encountered earlier. Let's take a quick tour of these building blocks.

An observable state

The state is at the epicenter of all things happening in the UI. MobX provides a core building block, called the **observable**, that represents the reactive state of your application. Any JavaScript object can be used to create an observable. We can use the aptly named observable() API as follows:

```
import {observable} from 'mobx';

let cart = observable({
    itemCount: 0,
    modified: new Date()
});
```

In the preceding example, we have created a simple `cart` object that is also an `observable`. The `observable()` API comes from the *mobx* NPM package. With this simple declaration of an `observable`, we now have a reactive `cart` that keeps track of changes happening on any of its properties: `itemCount` and `modified`.

Observing the state changes

Observables alone cannot make an interesting system. We also need their counterparts, the **observers**. MobX gives you three different kinds of observers, each tailor-made for the use cases you will encounter in your application. The core observers are `autorun`, `reaction`, and `when`. We will look at each of them in more detail in the next chapter, but let's introduce `autorun` for now.

The `autorun` API takes a function as its input and executes it immediately. It also keeps track of the observables that are used inside the passed-in function. When these tracked observables change, the function is re-executed. What is really beautiful and elegant about this simple setup is that there is no extra work required to track observables and subscribe to any changes. It all just happens automatically. It's not magic, per se, but definitely an intelligent system at work, which we will cover in a later section:

```
import {observable, autorun} from 'mobx';

let cart = observable({
    itemCount: 0,
    modified: new Date()
});

autorun(() => {
    console.log(`The Cart contains ${cart.itemCount} item(s).`);
});

cart.itemCount++;

// Console output:
The Cart contains 0 item(s).
The Cart contains 1 item(s).
```

In the preceding example, the `arrow-function` that was passed into `autorun` is executed for the first time and also when `itemCount` is incremented. This results in two console logs being printed. `autorun` makes the passed-in function (the *tracking-function*) an *observer* of the *observables* it references. In our case, `cart.itemCount` was being observed and when it was incremented, the *tracking* function was automatically notified, resulting in the console logs getting printed.

It's time to take action

Although we are mutating `cart.itemCount` directly, it is definitely not the recommended approach. Remember that the state should not be changed directly and instead should be done via *actions*. The use of an *action* also adds vocabulary to the operations that can be performed on the observable state.

In our case, we can call the state mutation that we were doing as an `incrementCount` action. Let's use the MobX `action` API to encapsulate the mutation:

```
import { observable, autorun, action } from 'mobx';

let cart = observable({
    itemCount: 0,
    modified: new Date(),
});

autorun(() => {
    console.log(`The Cart contains ${cart.itemCount} item(s).`);
});

const incrementCount = action(() => {
    cart.itemCount++;
});

incrementCount();
```

The `action` API takes a function that will be called whenever the action is invoked. It may seem superfluous that we are passing a function into *action*, when we could just wrap the mutation inside a plain function and call the plain function instead. An astute thought, for sure. Well, there is a good reason for that. Internally, `action` is doing much more than being a simple wrapper. It ensures that all notifications for state changes are fired, but only after the completion of the `action` function.

When you are modifying a lot of observables inside your action, you don't want to be notified about every little change immediately. Instead, you want to be able to wait for all changes to complete and then fire the notifications. This makes the system more performant and also reduces the noise of too many notifications, too soon.

Going back to our example, we can see that wrapping it in an action also improves the readability of the code. By giving a specific name to the action (incrementCount) we have added vocabulary to our domain. In doing so, we can abstract the details of what is needed to actually *increment the count*.

Observables, observers, and actions are at the core of MobX. With these fundamental concepts, we can build some of the most powerful and complex React applications.

> In the MobX literature, *side effects* are also called *reactions*. Unlike *actions* that *cause* state changes, *reactions* are the ones responding to state changes.

Note the striking similarity with the uni-directional data flow that we saw earlier. **Observables** capture the state of your application. **Observers** (also called *reactions*) include both the *side effect* handlers as well as the UI. The **actions** are, well, actions that cause a change in the observable state:

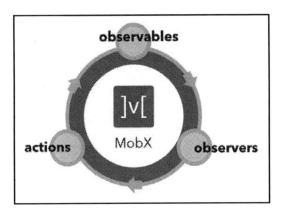

A comparison with Redux

If we were to talk about state management in React and we didn't mention Redux, it would be a complete remiss. Redux is an extremely popular state management library and its popularity stems from the fact that it simplified the original Flux architecture that was proposed by Facebook. It got rid of certain actors in Flux, such as *dispatchers*, which resulted in combining all the stores into one, commonly referred to as the **single state tree**.

 In this section, we will do a head-on comparison with another state management library called **Redux**. If you have *not* used Redux before, you can certainly skip this section and move on to this chapter's summary.

MobX has some conceptual similarities with Redux as far as the data flow is concerned, but that is also where the similarities end. The mechanism adopted by MobX is drastically different than the one taken by Redux. Let's have a brief overview of Redux before we get into a slightly deeper-level comparison.

Redux in a nutshell

The data flow triad that we saw earlier is also applicable to Redux in its entirety. It's in the *state update* mechanism that Redux adds its own twist. This can be seen in the following figure:

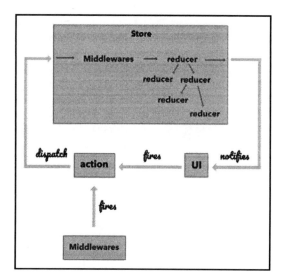

When the UI fires the action, it is dispatched on the store. Inside the store, the action first passes through one or more **middleware**, where it can get acted upon and swallowed without further propagation. If the action passes through the middleware, it is sent to one or more **reducers**, where it can be processed to produce a new state of the store.

This new state of the store is notified to all of the subscribers, with the **UI** being one of them. If the state is different from the previous value that the UI has, the UI is re-rendered and brought in sync with the new state.

There are few things here that are worth highlighting:

- From the point where the action enters the store, until the new state is computed, the entire process is synchronous.
- Reducers are pure functions that take in the action and the previous state and produce the new state. Since they are pure functions, you cannot put *side effects*, such as a network call, inside a reducer.
- Middleware is the only place where side effects can be performed, eventually resulting in an action being dispatched on the store.

If you are using Redux with React, which is the most likely combination, there is a utility library called `react-redux`, which can glue the store with React components. It does this through a function called `connect()`, which binds the store with the passed in React component. Inside `connect()`, the React component subscribes to the store for state-change notifications. Binding to the store via `connect()` means that every state change is notified to every component. This requires adding additional abstractions, such as a *state-selector* (using `mapStateToProps`) or implementing `shouldComponentUpdate()` to receive only the relevant state updates:

```
connect(mapStateToProps, mapDispatchToProps, mergeProps,
    options)(Component)
```

We are deliberately skipping over a few other details that are required for a complete React-Redux setup, but the essentials are in place for a deeper comparison of Redux with MobX.

MobX versus Redux

In principle, MobX and Redux accomplish the same goal of providing a uni-directional data flow. The *store* is the central actor that manages all state changes and notifies the UI and other observers of the change in state. The mechanism to achieve that is quite different between MobX and Redux.

Redux relies on *immutable* state snapshots and reference-comparisons between two state snapshots to check for changes. In contrast, MobX thrives on *mutable* state and uses a granular notification system to track state changes. This fundamental difference in approach has implications on the **Developer eXperience (DX)** of using each framework. We will use the DX of building a single feature to perform a MobX versus Redux comparison.

Let's start with Redux first. Here is the list of things you have to do when working with Redux:

- Define the shape of the state tree that will be encapsulated in the store. This is normally called `initialState`.
- Identify all actions that can be performed to change this state tree. Each action is defined in the form `{ type: string, payload: any }`. The `type` property is used to identify the action and `payload` is additional data that is carried along with the action. The action types are usually created as `string` constants and exported from a module.
- Defining raw actions every time you need to dispatch them becomes very verbose. Instead, the convention is to have an `action-creator` function that wraps the details of the action type and takes in the payload as an argument.

- Use the `connect` method to wire the React component with the store. Since every state change is notified to every component, you have to be careful to not re-render your component unnecessarily. The render should only happen when the part of the state that the component actually renders has changed (via `mapStateToProps`). Since every state change is notified to all *connected components*, it might be expensive to compute `mapStateToProps` every single time. To minimize these computations, it is recommended to use state selector libraries such as *reselect*. This increases the effort required to properly set up a performant React component. If you don't use these libraries, you have to take the onus of writing an efficient `shouldComponentUpdate` hook for the React component.

- Inside every reducer, you have to make sure that you are always returning a new instance of the state anytime there is a change. Note that the reducers are usually kept separate from the `initialState` definition and that requires going back and forth to ensure the proper state is changed in each of the reducer actions.

- Any side effect you want to perform has to be wrapped in middleware. For more complex side effects which involve async operations, it is better to rely on dedicated middleware libraries, such as `redux-thunk`, `redux-saga`, or `redux-observables`. Note that this also complicates how side effects are constructed and executed. Each of the previously mentioned middleware have their own conventions and terminology. Additionally, the place where an action is dispatched is not co-located with the place where the actual side effect is handled. This results in more jumping around files to construct the mental model of how a feature is put together.

- As the complexity of the feature increases, there is more fragmentation between `actions`, `action-creators`, `middlewares`, `reducers`, and `initialState`. Not having things co-located also increases the effort needed to develop a crisp mental model of a how a feature is put together.

In the MobX world, the developer experience is quite different. You will see more of this as we explore MobX throughout this book, but here is the top-level scoop:

- Define the observable state for the feature in a store class. The various properties that can be changed and should be observed are marked with the `observable` API.
- Define `actions` that will be needed to mutate the observable state.
- Define all of the side effects (`autorun`, `reaction` and `when`) within the same feature class. The co-location of actions, reactions, and the observable state keeps the mental model crisp. MobX also supports async state updates out of the box, so no additional middleware libraries are needed to manage it.
- Use the `mobx-react` package that includes the `observer` API, which allows the React components to connect to the observable store. You can sprinkle *observer* components throughout your React component tree, which is in fact the recommended approach to fine-tune component updates.
- The advantage of using the *observer* is that there is no extra work needed to make the component efficient. Internally, the *observer* API ensures that the component is only updated when the rendered observable state changes.

MobX shifts your mindset to think of the observable state and the corresponding React components. You don't have to focus much on the wiring needed to achieve this. It is abstracted away behind simple and elegant APIs, such as `observable`, `action`, `autorun`, and `observer`.

We can go as far as saying that MobX enables a more *declarative form* of Redux. There are no action creators, reducers, or middleware to handle actions and produce the new state. The actions, side effects (reactions), and observable state are co-located inside the class or module. There are no complex `connect()` methods to glue a React component to the store. A simple `observer()` does the job with no extra wiring.

 MobX is declarative Redux. It takes the workflow associated with Redux and simplifies it considerably. Some explicit setup is no longer needed, such as the use of `connect()` in Container components, reselect for memoized state selection, actions, reducers and of course the middleware.

Summary

The UI is the visual equivalent of data (the state) along with interactive controls to change that state. The UI fires actions, which leads to the change in state. *Side effects* are external operations that are triggered due to some state change. There are *observers* in the system that look out for certain state changes and perform the corresponding side effects.

The data flow triad of *Action --> State --> UI*, coupled with side effects, creates a simple mental model of the UI. MobX strongly adheres to this mental model and you can see that reflected in its API, with *observables, actions, reactions,* and *observers*. The simplicity of this API makes it easy to tackle some of the complex interactions in UI.

If you have used Redux before, you can see that MobX reduces the ceremony needed to cause a state change and handle side effects. MobX strives to provide a declarative and reactive API for state management without compromising on simplicity. Throughout this book, this philosophy of MobX will be explored, with a deeper look at its API and real-world use cases.

In the next chapter, we will dive into the world of MobX with a first hand look at its core building blocks.

2
Observables, Actions, and Reactions

Describing the structure of the client state is the first step in UI development. With MobX, you do this by creating your tree of **observables**. As the user interacts with the app, actions are invoked on your observable state, which in turn can cause reactions (aka side-effects). Continuing from Chapter 1, *Introduction to State Management*, we will now take a deeper look at the core concepts of MobX.

The topics covered in this chapter include:

- Creating the various kinds of observables
- Setting up the actions that mutate the observables
- Using reactions to handle external changes

Technical requirements

You will be required to have JavaScript programming language. Finally, to use the Git repository of this book, the user needs to install Git.

The code files of this chapter can be found on GitHub:
https://github.com/PacktPublishing/MobX-Quick-Start-Guide/tree/master/src/Chapter02

Check out the following video to see the code in action:
http://bit.ly/2NEww85

Observables

Data is the lifeblood of your UI. Going back to the equation that defines the relationship between data and UI, we know that the following is true:

$$UI = fn(State)$$

So, it makes sense to focus on *defining the structure* of data that will drive the UI. In MobX, we do this with the observables. Take a look at this diagram:

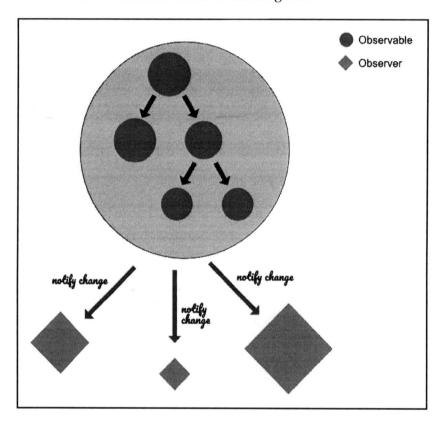

Observables, as the name suggests, are entities that can be observed. They keep track of changes happening to their values and notify all the *observers*. This seemingly simple behavior has powerful implications when you start designing the structure of your client-state. In the preceding diagram, every circle represents an **Observable**, and every diamond is an **Observer**. An observer can observe one or more observables and get notified when any of them change value.

Creating observables

The simplest way to create an observable is to use the `observable()` function. Take a look at the following:

```
const item = observable({
    name: 'Party Balloons',
    itemId: '1234',
    quantity: 2,
    price: 10,
    coupon: {
        code: 'BIGPARTY',
        discountPercent: 50
    }
});
```

`item` is now an `observable` object and will start tracking changes to its properties. You can use this object as a regular JavaScript object without any special API to *get* or *set* its values. In the preceding snippet, you can also create an observable `item` using `observable.object()`.

In the following snippet, we can see simple mutations made to the observables, like any regular JavaScript code:

```
// Set values
item.quantity += 3;
item.name = 'Small Balloons';

// Get values
console.log(`Buying ${item.quantity} of ${item.name}`);
```

Observable objects only track the properties provided in the initial value given to `observable()` or `observable.object()`. This means if you add new properties later, they will not become observable automatically. This is an important characteristic to remember about observable objects. They are like records or classes with a fixed set of attributes. If you do need dynamic tracking of properties, you should consider using *observable maps*; these will be covered further ahead in the chapter.

 Internally, MobX takes care of transparently tracking the property changes and notifying the corresponding observers. We will look into this internal behavior in a later chapter.

The `observable()` function automatically converts an *object*, an *array*, or a *map* into an observable entity. This automatic conversion is *not applied* for other types of data—such as JavaScript primitives (number, string, boolean, null, undefined), functions, or for class-instances (objects with prototypes). So, if you call `observable(20)`, it will fail with an error, as shown here:

```
Error: [mobx] The provided value could not be converted into an observable.
If you want just create an observable reference to the object use
'observable.box(value)'
```

As suggested in the error, we have to use the more specialized `observable.box()` to convert primitive values into an observable. Observables that wrap *primitives, functions,* or *class-instances* are called **boxed observables**. Take a look at this:

```
const count = observable.box(20);

// Get the count
console.log(`Count is ${count.get()}`);

// Change count
count.set(22);
```

We have to use the `get()` and `set()` methods of a boxed observable instead of directly reading or assigning to it. These methods give us the observability that is inherent to MobX.

Besides objects and singular values, you can also create observables out of arrays and maps. They have a corresponding API, as can be seen in this table:

objects	observable.object({ })
arrays	observable.array([ ])
maps	observable.map(value)
primitives, functions, class-instances	observable.box(value)

As we mentioned earlier, `observable()` will automatically convert an object, array, or a map into an observable. It is shorthand for `observable.object()`, `observable.array()`, or `observable.map()`, respectively. For primitives, functions, and class-instances, you should use the `observable.box()` API. Although, in practice, the use of `observable.box()` is fairly rare. It is more common to use `observable.object()`, `observable.array()`, or `observable.map()`.

MobX applies *deep observability* when creating an observable. This means MobX will automatically observe every property, at every level, in the object-tree, array, or map. It also tracks additions or removals in the cases of arrays and maps. This behavior works well for most scenarios but could be excessive in some cases. There are special decorators that you can apply to control this observability. We will look into this in Chapter 4, *Crafting the Observable Tree*.

Observable arrays

Using observable.array() is very similar to using an observable(). You pass an array as initial value or start with an empty array. In the following code example, we are starting with an empty array:

```
const items = observable.array(); // Start with empty array

console.log(items.length); // Prints: 0

items.push({
    name: 'hats', quantity: 40,
});

// Add one in the front
items.unshift({ name: 'Ribbons', quantity: 2 });

// Add at the back
items.push({ name: 'balloons', quantity: 1 });

console.log(items.length); // Prints: 3
```

Do note that the observable array is *not* a real JavaScript array, even though it has the same API as a JS Array. When you are passing this array to other libraries or APIs, you can convert it into a JS Array by calling toJS(), as shown here:

```
import { observable, toJS } from 'mobx';

const items = observable.array();

/* Add/remove items*/

const plainArray = toJS(items);
console.log(plainArray);
```

MobX will apply deep observability to observable arrays, which means it will track additions and removals of items from the array and also track property changes happening to each item in the array.

Observable maps

You can make an observable map with the `observable.map()` API. In principle, it works the same way as `observable.array()` and `observable.object()`, but it is meant for ES6 Maps. The observable map instance shares the same API as a regular ES6 Map. Observable maps are great for tracking dynamic changes to the keys and values. This is in stark contrast to observable objects, which do not track properties that are added after creation.

In the following code example, we are creating a dynamic dictionary of Twitter-handles to names. This is a great fit for an observable map, as we are *adding* keys after creation. Take a look at this code block:

```
import { observable } from 'mobx';

// Create an Observable Map
const twitterUserMap = observable.map();

console.log(twitterUserMap.size); // Prints: 0

// Add keys
twitterUserMap.set('pavanpodila', 'Pavan Podila');
twitterUserMap.set('mweststrate', 'Michel Weststrate');

console.log(twitterUserMap.get('pavanpodila')); // Prints: Pavan Podila
console.log(twitterUserMap.has('mweststrate')); // Prints: Michel
Weststrate

twitterUserMap.forEach((value, key) => console.log(`${key}: ${value}`));

// Prints:
// pavanpodila: Pavan Podila
// mweststrate: Michel Weststrate
```

A note on observability

When you use the `observable()` API, MobX will apply *deep observability* to the observable instance. This means it will track changes happening to the observable object, array, or map and do it for every property, at every level. In the cases of arrays and maps, it will also track the additions and removals of entries. Any new entry in an array or a map is also made into a deep observable. This is definitely a great sensible default and works well for most situations. However, there will be cases where you may not want this default.

You can change this behavior at the time of creating the observable. Instead of using `observable()`, you can use the sibling APIs (`observable.object()`, `observable.array()`, `observable.map()`) to create the observable. Each of these takes an extra argument for setting options on the observable instance. Take a look at this:

```
observable.object(value, decorators, { deep: false });
observable.map(values, { deep: false });
observable.array(values, { deep: false });
```

By passing in `{ deep: false }` as an option, you can effectively *prune* the observability just to the first level. This means the following:

For observable objects, MobX only observes the initial set of properties. If the value of property is an object, an array, or a map, it won't do any further observation.

> Note that the `{ deep: false }` option is the third argument for `observable.object()`. The second argument, called **decorators**, gives you more fine-grained control over the observability. We will be covering this in a later chapter. For now, you can just pass an empty object as the second argument.

For observable arrays, MobX only observes the addition and removal of items in the array. If an item is an object, an array, or a map, it won't do any further observation.

For observable maps, MobX only observes the addition and removal of items in the map. If the value of a key is an object, an array, or a map, it won't do any further observation.

Now, it is worth mentioning that `observable()` internally calls one of the preceding APIs and sets the option to `{ deep: true }`. This is the reason `observable()` has deep observability.

The computed observable

The observables we have seen so far have a direct correspondence with the shape of the client-state. If you are representing a list of items, you would use an observable array in your client-state. Similarly, each item in a list can be an observable object or an observable map. The story does not stop there. MobX gives you yet another kind of observable, called a **computed property** or a **computed observable**.

A computed property is not an observable that is inherent to the client state. Instead, it is an observable that *derives its value* from other observables. Now, *why would that be useful?* you may ask. Let's take an example to see the benefits.

Consider the `cart` observable, which tracks a list of items. Take a look at this:

```
import { observable } from 'mobx';

const cart = observable.object({
    items: [],
    modified: new Date(),
});
```

Let's say you want to have a `description` property that describes the `cart` in this format: There `{is, are} {no, one, n} item{s}` in the cart.

For zero items, the description says this: *There are no items in the cart.*

When there is only one item, the description becomes this: *There is one item in the cart.*

For two or more items *(n)*, the description should be: *There are n items in the cart.*

Let's ponder how we can go about modeling this property. Consider the following:

- Clearly, the `description` is not an inherent property of the cart. Its value depends on `items.length`.
- We can add an observable property called `description`, but then we have to update it anytime `items` or `items.length` changes. That is extra work and easy to forget. Also, we run the risk of someone modifying the description from the outside.
- Description should just be a getter with no setter. If someone is observing description, they should be notified anytime it changes.

As you can tell from the preceding analysis, we can't seem to fit this behavior into any of the previously-discussed observable types. What we need here is the computed property. We can define a *computed* description property by simply adding a `get-property` to the `cart` observable. It will derive its value from `items.length`. Take a look at this code block:

```
const cart = observable.object({
    items: [],
    modified: new Date(),

    get description() {
        switch (this.items.length) {
            case 0:
                return 'There are no items in the cart';
            case 1:
                return 'There is one item in the cart';
            default:
                return `There are ${this.items.length} items in the
                cart`;
        }
    },
});
```

Now, you can simply read `cart.description` and always get the latest description. Anyone observing this property would be automatically notified when `cart.description` changes, which will happen if you add or remove items from the cart.The following is an example of how this computed property can be used:

```
cart.items.push({ name: 'Shoes', quantity: 1 });
console.log(cart.description);
```

 Note that it also satisfies all of the criteria from the previous brainstorming on the `description` property. I'll let you, the reader, confirm this is the case.

Computed properties, also known as **derivations**, are one of the most powerful tools in the MobX toolbox. By thinking of your client-state in terms of a minimal set of observables and augmenting it with derivations (computed properties), you can model a variety of scenarios effortlessly. Computed properties derive their value from other observables. If any of these depending observables change, the computed property changes as well.

You can build a computed property out of other computed properties too. MobX internally builds a dependency tree to keep track of the observables. It also caches the value of the computed property to avoid unnecessary computation. This is an important characteristic that greatly improves the performance of the MobX reactivity system. Unlike JavaScript get properties, which are always eagerly evaluated, computed properties memoize (aka cache) the value and only evaluate when the dependent observables change.

As you develop experience using MobX, you will realize that *computed properties* are possibly your best observable-friends.

Better syntax with decorators

All of our examples so far have used the *ES5 API* of MobX. However, there is a special form of the API, which gives us a very convenient way of expressing the observables. This is made possible with the `@decorator` syntax.

The decorator syntax is still a pending proposal (as of this writing) for inclusion in the JavaScript language standard. But that doesn't stop us from using it, as we have **Babel** to help us out. By using the Babel plugin, `transform-decorators-legacy`, we can transpile the decorator syntax into regular ES5 code. If you are using TypeScript, you can also enable decorator support by setting your `{ experimentalDecorators: true}` compiler option in your `tsconfig.json`.

The decorator syntax is *only available for classes* and can be used for class declarations, properties and methods. Here is an equivalent `Cart` observable, expressed with decorators:

```
class Cart {
    @observable.shallow items = [];
    @observable modified = new Date();

    @computed get description() {
        switch (this.items.length) {
            case 0:
                return 'There are no items in the cart';
            case 1:
                return 'There is one item in the cart';
            default:
                return `There are ${this.items.length} items in the
                cart`;
        }
    }
}
```

Notice the use of decorators to *decorate* the observable properties. The default @observable decorator does deep observation on all the properties of the value. It is actually a shorthand for using @observable.deep.

Similarly, we have the @observable.shallow decorator, which is a *rough* equivalent of setting the { deep: false } option on the observable. It works for objects, arrays, and maps. We will cover the more technically correct ES5 equivalent of observable.shallow in Chapter 4 , *Crafting the Observable Tree.*

The snippet below shows the items and metadata properties, marked as *shallow observables*:

```
class Cart {
    // Using decorators
    @observable.shallow items = [];
    @observable.shallow metadata = {};
}
```

We will be covering a few more decorators in a later chapter, but we did not want to wait until then to discuss the decorator syntax. We definitely think you should pick decorators as your first choice for declaring observables. Note that they are only available inside classes. However, the vast majority of the time, you will be using classes to model your observable tree, so decorators greatly help in making it more readable.

Actions

Although you can change an observable directly, it is highly recommended that you use *actions* to do it. If you remember, in the previous chapter, we saw that actions are the ones that cause a state-change. The UI simply fires the actions and expects some observables to be mutated. Actions hide the details of how the mutation should happen or what observables should be affected.

The diagram below is a reminder that **UI** can modify the **State** only via an **Action**:

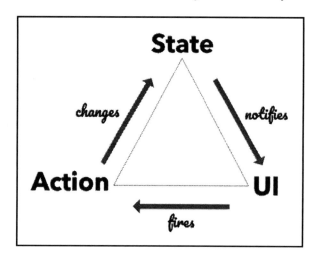

Actions introduce *vocabulary* into the UI and give declarative names to the operations that mutate the state. MobX embraces this idea completely and makes actions a *first-class* concept. To create an action, we simply wrap the mutating function inside the `action()` API. This gives us back a function that can be invoked just like the original passed-in function. Take a look at this code block:

```
import { observable, action } from 'mobx';

const cart = observable({
    items: [],
    modified: new Date(),
});

// Create the actions
const addItem = action((name, quantity) => {
    const item = cart.items.find(x => x.name === name);
    if (item) {
        item.quantity += 1;
    } else {
```

```
        cart.items.push({ name, quantity });
    }

    cart.modified = new Date();
});

const removeItem = action(name => {
    const item = cart.items.find(x => x.name === name);
    if (item) {
        item.quantity -= 1;

        if (item.quantity <= 0) {
            cart.items.remove(item);
        }

        cart.modified = new Date();
    }
});

// Invoke actions
addItem('balloons', 2);
addItem('paint', 2);
removeItem('paint');
```

In the preceding snippet, we have introduced two actions: addItem() and removeItem(), which add and remove an item to and from the cart observable. Since action() returns a function that forwards arguments to the passed-in function, we can invoke addItem() and removeItem() with the required arguments.

Besides improving the readability of the code, actions also boost performance of MobX. By default, when you modify an observable, MobX will *immediately* fire a notification for the change. If you are modifying a bunch of observables together, you would rather fire the change notifications after all of them are modified. This would reduce the noise of too many notifications and also treat the set of changes as one *atomic transaction*. These are, in essence, the core responsibilities of an action().

Enforcing the use of actions

It should come as no surprise that MobX strongly recommends using *actions* for modifying observables. In fact, this can be made mandatory by configuring MobX to always enforce this policy, also called the **strict mode**. The configure() function can be used to set the enforceActions option to true. MobX will now throw an error if you try to modify an observable outside of an action.

Going back to our previous example with cart, if we try to modify it *outside* an *action*, MobX will fail with an error, as you can see from the following example:

```
import { observable, configure } from 'mobx';

configure({
    enforceActions: true,
});

// Modifying outside of an action
cart.items.push({ name: 'test', quantity: 1 });
cart.modified = new Date();

Error: [mobx] Since strict-mode is enabled, changing observed observable
values outside actions is not allowed. Please wrap the code in an `action`
if this change is intended. Tried to modify: ObservableObject@1.items
```

 There is one little thing to remember regarding the use of configure({ enforceActions: true }): It will only throw errors if there are observers watching the observables that you are trying to mutate. If there are no observers for those observables, MobX will safely ignore it. This is because there is no risk of triggering reactions too early. However, if you do want to be strict about this, you can also set { enforceActions: 'strict' }. This will throw an error even if there are no observers attached to the mutating observables.

Decorating actions

The use of decorators is pervasive in MobX. Actions also get special treatment with the @action decorator to mark class methods as actions. With decorators, the Cart class can be written as shown here:

```
class Cart {
    @observable modified = new Date();
    @observable.shallow items = [];

    @action
    addItem(name, quantity) {
        this.items.push({ name, quantity });
        this.modified = new Date();
    }

    @action.bound
    removeItem(name) {
```

```
        const item = this.items.find(x => x.name === name);
        if (item) {
            item.quantity -= 1;

            if (item.quantity <= 0) {
                this.items.remove(item);
            }
        }
    }
}
```

In the preceding snippet, we used `@action.bound` for the `removeItem()` action. This is a special form that pre-binds the instance of the class to the method. This means you can pass around the reference to `removeItem()` and be assured that the `this` value always points to the instance of the Cart.

A different way of declaring the `removeItem` action with a pre-bound `this` is with the use of class properties and arrow-functions. This can be seen in the following code:

```
class Cart {
    /* ... */
    @action removeItem = (name) => {
        const item = this.items.find(x => x.name === name);
        if (item) {
            item.quantity -= 1;

            if (item.quantity <= 0) {
                this.items.remove(item);
            }
        }
    }
}
```

Here, `removeItem` is a *class-property* whose value is an *arrow-function*. Because of the *arrow-function*, it binds to the *lexical* `this`, which is the instance of the `Cart`.

Reactions

Reactions can really change the world for your app. They are the side-effect causing behaviors that react to the changes in observables. Reactions complete the core triad of MobX and act as the observers of the observables. Take a look at this diagram:

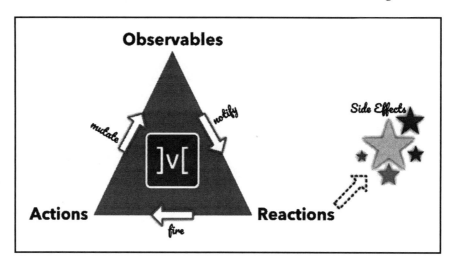

MobX gives you three different ways to express your reactions or side-effects. These are `autorun()`, `reaction()`, and `when()`. Let's see each of these in turn.

autorun()

`autorun()` is a long-running side-effect that takes in a function (`effect-function`) as its argument. The `effect-function` function is where you apply all your side-effects. Now, these side-effects may depend on one or more observables. MobX will automatically keep track of any change happening to these *dependent* observables and re-execute this function to apply the side-effect. It's easier to see this in code, as shown here:

```
import { observable, action, autorun } from 'mobx';

class Cart {
    @observable modified = new Date();
    @observable.shallow items = [];

    constructor() {
        autorun(() => {
            console.log(`Items in Cart: ${this.items.length}`);
```

```
        });
    }

    @action
    addItem(name, quantity) {
        this.items.push({ name, quantity });
        this.modified = new Date();
    }
}

const cart = new Cart();
cart.addItem('Power Cable', 1);
cart.addItem('Shoes', 1);

// Prints:
// Items in Cart: 0
// Items in Cart: 1
// Items in Cart: 2
```

In the preceding example we are logging an *observable* (`this.items.length`) to the console. The logging happens *immediately* and also any time the observable changes. This is the defining characteristic of `autorun()`; it runs immediately and also on every change to the dependent observables.

We mentioned earlier that `autorun()` is a long-running side-effect and continues as long as you don't explicitly stop it. But then, how do you actually stop it? Well, the return-value of `autorun()` is a function that is in fact a `disposer-function`. By calling it, you can cancel the `autorun()` side-effect. Take a look at this:

```
import { observable, action, autorun } from 'mobx';

class Cart {
    /* ... */

    cancelAutorun = null;

    constructor() {
        this.cancelAutorun = autorun(() => {
            console.log(`Items in Cart: ${this.items.length}`);
        });
    }
    /* ... */
}

const cart = new Cart();
// 1. Cancel the autorun side-effect
cart.cancelAutorun();
```

```
// 2. The following will not cause any logging to happen
cart.addItem('Power Cable', 1);
cart.addItem('Shoes', 1);

// Prints:
// Items in Cart: 0
```

In the preceding snippet, we are storing the return-value of `autorun()` (a `disposer-function`) in a class property: `cancelAutorun`. By invoking it just after instantiating `Cart`, we have canceled the side-effect. Now `autorun()` only prints once, and never again.

 Quick Reader Question: Why does it print only once? Since we are cancelling immediately, shouldn't `autorun()` skip printing altogether? The answer to this is to refresh the core characteristic of `autorun`.

reaction()

`reaction()` is yet another kind of reaction in MobX. Yes, the choice of the API name was intentional. `reaction()` is similar to `autorun()` but waits for a change in the observables before executing the `effect-function`. `reaction()` in fact takes two arguments, which are as follows:

reaction(tracker-function, effect-function): disposer-function

tracker-function: () => data, **effect-function**: (data) => {}

`tracker-function` is where all the observables are tracked. Any time the tracked observables change, it will re-execute. It is supposed to return a value that is used to compare it to the previous run of `tracker-function`. If these return-values differ, the `effect-function` is executed.

By breaking up the activity of a reaction into a change-detecting function (`tracker` function) and the `effect` function, `reaction()` gives us more fine-grained control over when a side-effect should be caused. It is no longer just dependent on the observables it is tracking inside the `tracker` function. Instead, it now depends on the data returned by the tracker function. The `effect` function receives this data in its input. Any observables used in the effect function are not tracked.

Just like `autorun()`, you also get a `disposer` function as the return-value of `reaction()`. This can be used to cancel the side-effect anytime you want.

We can put this into practice with an example. Let's say you want to be notified anytime an item in your `Cart` changes its price. After all, you don't want to purchase something that suddenly shoots up in price. At the same time, you don't want to miss out on a great deal as well. So, getting a notification when the price changes is a useful thing to have. We can implement this by using `reaction()`, as shown here:

```
import { observable, action, reaction } from 'mobx';

class Cart {
    @observable modified = new Date();
    @observable items = [];

    cancelPriceTracker = null;

    trackPriceChangeForItem(name) {
        if (this.cancelPriceTracker) {
            this.cancelPriceTracker();
        }

        // 1. Reaction to track price changes
        this.cancelPriceTracker = reaction(
            () => {
                const item = this.items.find(x => x.name === name);
                return item ? item.price : null;
            },
            price => {
                console.log(`Price changed for ${name}: ${price !==
                null ? price : 0}`);
            },
        );
    }

    @action
    addItem(name, price) {
        this.items.push({ name, price });
        this.modified = new Date();
    }

    @action
    changePrice(name, price) {
        const item = this.items.find(x => x.name === name);
        if (item) {
            item.price = price;
        }
    }
```

```
    }
}

const cart = new Cart();

cart.addItem('Shoes', 20);

// 2. Now track price for "Shoes"
cart.trackPriceChangeForItem('Shoes');

// 3. Change the price
cart.changePrice('Shoes', 100);
cart.changePrice('Shoes', 50);

// Prints:
// Price changed for Shoes: 100
// Price changed for Shoes: 50
```

In the preceding snippet, we are setting up a price tracker in *comment 1*, as a *reaction to track price changes*. Notice that it takes two functions as inputs. The first function (`tracker-function`) finds the item with the given `name` and returns its price as the output of the `tracker` function. Any time it changes, the corresponding `effect` function is executed.

The console logs also print only when the price changes. This is exactly the behavior we wanted and achieved through a `reaction()`. Now that you are notified of the price changes, you can make better buying decisions.

A reactive UI

On the topic of reactions, it is worth mentioning that the UI is one of the most glorious reactions (or side-effect) you can have in an app. As we saw in the earlier chapter, *UI* depends on data and applies a transformation function to generate the visual representation. In the MobX world, this UI is also reactive, in the sense that it reacts to the changes in data and automatically re-renders itself.

MobX provides a companion library called ***mobx-react*** that has bindings to React. By using a decorator function (`observer()`) from `mobx-react`, you can transform a react component to observe the observables used in the `render()` function. When they change, a re-render of the react component is triggered. Internally, `observer()` creates a wrapper component that uses a plain `reaction()` to watch the observables and re-render as a side-effect. This is why we treat UI as being just another side-effect, albeit a very visible and obvious one.

A short example of using `observer()` is shown next. We are using a **stateless functional component,** which we are passing to the observer. Since we are reading the `item` observable, the component will now react to changes in `item`. After two seconds, when we update `item`, the `ItemComponent` will automatically re-render. Take a look at this:

```
import { observer } from 'mobx-react';
import { observable } from 'mobx';
import ReactDOM from 'react-dom';
import React from 'react';

const item = observable.box(30);

// 1. Create the component with observer
const ItemComponent = observer(() => {
    // 2. Read an observable: item
    return <h1>Current Item Value = {item.get()}</h1>;
});

ReactDOM.render(<ItemComponent />, document.getElementById('root'));

// 3. Update item
setTimeout(() => item.set(50), 2000);
```

We will cover `mobx-react` in Chapter 3, *A React App with MobX,* and also throughout this book.

when()

As the name suggests, when() only executes the effect-function *when a condition is met* and automatically disposes the side-effect after that. Thus, when() is a one-time side-effect compared to autorun() and reaction(), which are long-running. The predicate function normally relies on some observables to do the conditional checks. If the observables change, the predicate function will be re-evaluated.

when() takes two arguments, which are as follows:

```
when(predicate-function, effect-function): disposer-function

predicate-function: () => boolean, effect-function: ()=>{}
```

The predicate function is expected to return a Boolean value. When it becomes true, the effect function is executed, and the when() is automatically disposed. Note that when() also gives you back a disposer function that you can call to prematurely cancel the side-effect.

In this following code block, we are monitoring the availability of an item and notifying the user when it is back in stock. This is the case of a one-time effect that you don't really have to continuously monitor. It's only when the item count in the inventory goes above zero, that you execute the side-effect of notifying the user. Take a look at this:

```
import { observable, action, when } from 'mobx';

class Inventory {
    @observable items = [];

    cancelTracker = null;

    trackAvailability(name) {
        // 1. Establish the tracker with when
        this.cancelTracker = when(
            () => {
                const item = this.items.find(x => x.name === name);
                return item ? item.quantity > 0 : false;
            },
            () => {
                console.log(`${name} is now available`);
            },
        );
    }

    @action
    addItem(name, quantity) {
```

```
        const item = this.items.find(x => x.name === name);
        if (item) {
            item.quantity += quantity;
        } else {
            this.items.push({ name, quantity });
        }
    }
}

const inventory = new Inventory();

inventory.addItem('Shoes', 0);
inventory.trackAvailability('Shoes');

// 2. Add two pairs
inventory.addItem('Shoes', 2);

// 3. Add one more pair
inventory.addItem('Shoes', 1);

// Prints:
// Shoes is now available
```

when() here takes two arguments. The predicate function returns true when the
item.quantity is greater than zero. The effect function simply notifies (via
console.log) that the item is available in the store. When the predicate becomes true,
when() executes the side-effect and automatically disposes itself. Thus, when we add two
pairs of shoes into the inventory, when() executes and logs the availability.

Notice that when we add one more pair of shoes into the inventory, no logs are printed.
This is because at this time when() has been disposed and is no longer monitoring the
availability of *Shoes*. This is the one-time effect of when().

when() with a promise

There is a special version of when(), which takes only one argument (the
predicate function), and gives back a promise instead of the disposer function. This is a
nice trick where you can skip using the effect function and instead wait for when() to
resolve before executing the effect. This is easier to see in code, as shown here:

```
class Inventory {
    /* ... */

    async trackAvailability(name) {
        // 1. Wait for availability
```

```
await when(() => {
    const item = this.items.find(x => x.name === name);
    return item ? item.quantity > 0 : false;
});

// 2. Execute side-effect
console.log(`${name} is now available`);
}

/* ... */
}
```

In *comment 1*, we are waiting for the availability of the item using when() that only takes the predicate function. By using the async-await operators to wait for the promise, we get clean, readable code. Any code that follows the await statement is automatically scheduled to execute after the promise resolves. This is a nicer form of using when() if you prefer *not* to pass an effect callback.

 when() is also very efficient and does not poll the predicate function to check for changes. Instead, it relies on the MobX reactivity system to re-evaluate the predicate function, when the underlying observables change.

Quick recap on reactions

MobX offers a couple of ways to execute side-effects, but you have to identify which one fits your needs. Here is a quick round-up that can help you in making the right choice.

We have three ways of running side-effects:

1. autorun(effect-function: () => {}): Useful for long-running side-effects. The effect function executes immediately and also anytime the dependent observables (used within it) change. It returns a disposer function that can be used to cancel anytime.
2. reaction(tracker-function: () => data, effect-function: (data) => {}): Also for long-running side-effects. It executes the effect function only when the data returned by the tracker function is different. In other words, reaction() waits for a change in the observables before any side-effects are run. It also gives back a disposer function to cancel the effect prematurely.

3. when(predicate-function: () => boolean, effect-function: () =>
   {}): Useful for one-off effects. The predicate function is evaluated anytime its
   dependent observables change. It executes the effect function only when the
   predicate function returns true. when() automatically disposes itself after
   running the effect function. There is a special form of when() that only takes in
   the predicate function and returns a promise. Use it with async-await for a
   simpler when().

Summary

The story of MobX revolves around observables. Actions mutate these observables.
Derivations and Reactions observe and react to changes to these observables. Observables,
actions, and reactions form the core triad.

We have seen several ways to shape your observables with objects, arrays, maps, and
boxed observables. Actions are the recommended way to modify observables. They add to
the vocabulary of operations and boost performance by minimizing change notifications.
Reactions are the observers that react to changes in observables. They are the ones causing
side-effects in the app.

Reactions come in three flavors, autorun(), reaction(), and when(), and distinguish
themselves as being long-running or one-time. when(), the only one-time effector, comes in
a simpler form, where it can return a promise, given a predicate function.

A React App with MobX 3

Working with React is fun. Now, couple that with MobX for all your state management needs, and you have a supercharged combination. With the basics of MobX out of the way, we can now venture into building a simple React app using the ideas discussed so far. We will tackle the process of defining an observable state, the actions that can be invoked on that state, and the React UI that will observe and render the changing state.

The topics covered in this chapter include the following:

- The book search use-case
- Creating the observable state and actions
- Building the Reactive UI

Technical requirements

You will be required to have JavaScript programming language. Finally, to use the Git repository of this book, the user needs to install Git.

The code files of this chapter can be found on GitHub:
`https://github.com/PacktPublishing/MobX-Quick-Start-Guide/tree/master/src/Chapter03`

Check out the following video to see the code in action:
`http://bit.ly/2vOHnkW`

The book search

The use-case for our simple React app is one from traditional e-commerce applications, that is, searching for a product in a giant inventory. In our case, the search is for books. We will use the *Goodreads* API to search for a book by title or author. Goodreads requires us to register an account to use their API.

Create a Goodreads account by visiting this URL: `https://www.` `goodreads.com/api/keys`. You can use your Amazon or Facebook account to log in. Once you have the account, you need to generate an API key to make the API calls.

Goodreads exposes a set of endpoints that give back the results in XML. Agreed, it's not ideal, but they have an extensive collection of books and it's a small price to pay to convert XML into a JSON object. In fact, we will use an `npm` package for this conversion. The endpoint we will be using is search-books (`https://www.goodreads.com/search/index.` `xml?key=API_KEYq=SEARCH_TERM`).

The UI for our app will look something like the following:

MobX QuickStart Book Store

Q javascript

Showing **20** of 2109 results.

JavaScript: The Good Parts
Douglas Crockford
4.23★ from **6855** ratings.

JavaScript Patterns
Stoyan Stefanov
4.16★ from **1383** ratings.

JavaScript: The Definitive Guide
David Flanagan
4.01★ from **2390** ratings.

Even in this fairly simple-looking interface, there are some non-trivial use-cases. Since we are making a network call to fetch the results, we have an intermediate state of *waiting-for-results* before we show the *list-of-results*. Also, the real world is harsh and your network call could fail or return zero results. All these states will be handled in our React UI with the help of MobX.

Observable state and actions

The UI is just a grandiose transformation of data. It is also an observer of this data and fires actions to change it. Since data (aka state) is so central to a UI, it makes sense we start first by modeling this state. With MobX, observables represent that state. Looking back at the UI design from before, we can identify various parts of the observable state:

- There is the search-text that the user types. This is an `observable` field of type string.
- There is an observable array of results.
- There is meta information about the results, such as the current subset and the total result count.
- There is some state to capture the `async search()` operation that we will be invoking. The initial `status` of the operation is `empty`. Once the user invokes the search, we are in the `pending` state. When the search completes, we could either be in the `completed` or `failed` state. This looks more like an enumeration of `<empty>`, `pending`, `completed`, or `failed`, and can be captured with an `observable` field.

Since all of these state properties are related, we could put them under one observable object:

```
const searchState = observable({
    term: '',
    state: '',
    results: [],
    totalCount: 0,
});
```

This is certainly a good start and seems to capture most of what we need to show on the UI. Besides the state, we also need to identify the operations that can be performed on the UI. For our simple UI, this includes invoking the search and updating the term as the user types characters into the text box. Operations in MobX are modeled as actions, which internally mutate the observable state. We can add these as *actions* on the searchState observable:

```
const searchState = observable({
    term: '',
    status: '',
    results: [],
    totalCount: 0,

    search: action(function() {
        // invoke search API
    }),

    setTerm: action(function(value) {
        this.term = value;
    }),
});
```

The searchState observable is slowly growing in size and also accumulating some syntactic-noise in defining the observable state. As we add more observable fields, computed properties and actions, this can definitely become more unwieldy. A better way to model this is to use classes and decorators.

 There is a little caveat with the way we have defined the actions for the searchState observable. Note that we have deliberately avoided the use of arrow-functions to define the action. This is because arrow-functions capture the **lexical this** at the time the action is defined. However, the observable() API returns a new object, which is of course different from the **lexical this** that is captured in the action() call. This means, the this that you are mutating would not be the object that is returned from observable(). You can try this out by passing arrow-functions into the action() calls.

By passing a plain-function into the action(), we can be assured that this would point to the correct instance of the observable.

Let's see how this looks with classes and decorators:

```
class BookSearchStore {
    @observable term = '';
    @observable status = '';
    @observable.shallow results = [];

    @observable totalCount = 0;

    @action.bound
    setTerm(value) {
        this.term = value;
    }

    @action.bound
    async search() {
        // invoke search API
    }
}

export const store = new BookSearchStore();
```

The use of decorators makes it easy to see the observable fields of the class. In fact, we have the flexibility to mix and match observable fields with regular fields. Decorators also make it easy to tweak the level of observability (for example: a `shallow` observable for the results). The `BookSearchStore` class captures the observable fields and actions with the help of decorators. Since we only need one instance of this class, we are exporting the singleton-instance as `store`.

Managing the async action

Things are more interesting with the `async search()` action. Our UI needs to know the exact state of the operation at any point in time. For that, we have the observable field: `status`, that keeps track of the operation state. It starts with the `empty` state initially and goes to `pending` at the beginning of the operation. Once the operation completes, it can either be in the `completed` or `failed` state. You can see this in the code, as follows:

```
class BookSearchStore {
    @observable term = '';
    @observable status = '';
    @observable.shallow results = [];

    @observable totalCount = 0;

    /* ... */
```

```
@action.bound
async search() {
    try {
        this.status = 'pending';
        const result = await searchBooks(this.term);

        runInAction(() => {
            this.totalCount = result.total;
            this.results = result.items;
            this.status = 'completed';
        });
    } catch (e) {
        runInAction(() => (this.status = 'failed'));
        console.log(e);
    }
}
}
```

A few things stand out in the preceding code:

- `async` actions are not very different from `sync` actions. In fact, an *async-action is just sync-actions at different points in time.*
- Setting the observable state is just a matter of assignment. We wrap the code after `await` in a `runInAction()` to ensure all observables are mutated inside an action. This becomes key when we turn on the `enforceActions` configuration for MobX.
- Because we are using `async-await`, we are handling the two future possibilities in one place.
- The `searchBooks()` function is just a service-method that makes the call to the Goodreads API and fetches the results. It returns a promise, which we `await` inside the `async` action.

At this point, we have the observable state of our app ready, along with the set of actions that can be performed on these observables. The UI that we will create is simply going to paint this observable state and expose controls to invoke the actions. Let's jump straight into the observer-land of UI.

One observation you can make in the `async search()` method just seen is the wrapping of the state mutation in `runInAction()`. This can get tedious if you have multiple `await` calls with state mutation in between those calls. Diligently wrapping each of those state-mutations can be cumbersome and you may even forget to wrap!

To avoid this unwieldy ceremony, you could use a utility function called `flow()`, which takes in a `generator` function and, instead of `await`, uses the `yield` operator. The `flow()` utility correctly wraps the state-mutations following a `yield` within `action()`, so you don't have to do it yourself. We will use this approach in a later chapter.

The Reactive UI

In the core-triad of MobX, reactions play the role of affecting the outside world. In Chapter 2, *Observables, Actions, and Reactions*, we have seen a few of these reactions in the form of `autorun()`, `reaction()`, and `when()`:

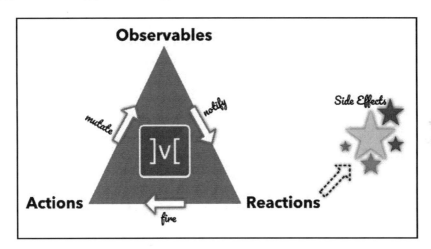

The `observer()` is yet another kind of reaction that helps in binding the React world to MobX. `observer()` is part of the `mobx-react` NPM package, a binding library for MobX and React. It creates a **higher-order-component (HOC)** that wraps a React component to automatically update on changes to the observable state. Internally, `observer()` keeps track of observables that are dereferenced in the `render` method of the component. When any of them change, a re-render of the component is triggered.

It is quite common to sprinkle `observer()` components throughout the UI component tree. Wherever an observable is required to render the component, an `observer()` can be used.

The UI that we want to build will map the observable state of the `BookSearchStore` to various components. Let's decompose the UI into its structural components, as seen in the following figure. The observer-components here include the **SearchTextField** and the **ResultsList**:

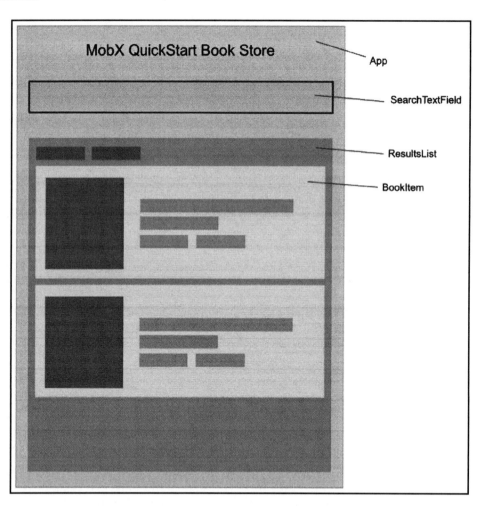

When you start out mapping the observable state to React components, you should start with one monolithic component that reads all the necessary state and renders it out. Then, you can start splitting the observer-components and gradually create the component hierarchy. It is recommended to get as granular as you can with your observer-components. This ensures React is not unnecessarily rendering the entire component when only a small part of it is changing.

At the highest level, we have the `App` component that composes the `SearchTextField` and `ResultsList`. In code, this looks as follows:

```
import {inject, observer} from 'mobx-react';

@inject('store')
@observer
class App extends React.Component {
    render() {
        const { store } = this.props;

        return (
            <Fragment>
                <Header />

                <Grid container>
                    <Grid item xs={12}>
                        <Paper elevation={2} style={{ padding: '1rem' }}>
                            <SearchTextField
                                onChange={this.updateSearchText}
                                onEnter={store.search}
                            />
                        </Paper>
                    </Grid>

                    <ResultsList style={{ marginTop: '2rem' }} />
                </Grid>
            </Fragment>
        );
    }

    updateSearchText = event => {
        this.props.store.setTerm(event.target.value);
    };
}
```

If it has caught your eye already, there is a new decorator on the App class that we have not seen before: inject('store'), also part of the mobx-react package. This creates a HOC that binds the store observable to the React component. This means that, inside the render() of the App component, we can expect a store property to be available on the props.

 We are using the material-ui NPM package for various UI components. This component library gives a material design look to our UI and provides many of the utility components, such as TextField, LinearProgress, Grid, and so on.

Getting to the store

Using inject(), you can connect the observable BookSearchStore to any of your React components. The mystery question, however, is: *How does* inject() *know about our* BookSearchStore? This is where you need to see what happens at one level above the App component, where we render the entire React app:

```
import { store } from './BookStore';
import React, { Fragment } from 'react';
import ReactDOM from 'react-dom';
import { Provider } from 'mobx-react';

ReactDOM.render(
    <Provider store={store}>
        <App />
    </Provider>,
    document.getElementById('root'),
);
```

The Provider component from mobx-react establishes the real connecting glue with the BookSearchStore observable. The exported singleton instance of BookSearchStore (named store), is passed as a prop named store into Provider. Internally, it uses the React Context to propagate the store to any component wrapped by the inject() decorator. Thus, the Provider provides the store observable and inject() connects to *React Context* (exposed by Provider), and injects the store into the wrapped component:

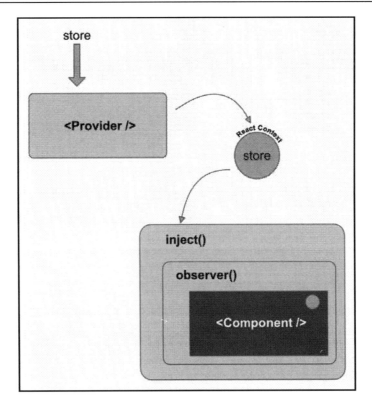

It is worth noting that there is nothing special about the named prop `store`. You can choose any name you like, and can even pass multiple observable instances into `Provider`. If our simple app needed a separate store for *user-preferences*, we could have passed it as follows:

```
import { store } from './BookStore';
import { preferences } from 'PreferencesStore;

<Provider store={store} userPreferences={preferences}>
    <App />
</Provider>
```

Of course, this means `inject()` will also be referencing this as `userPreferences`:

```
@inject('userPreferences')
@observer
class PreferencesViewer extends React.Component {
    render() {
        const { userPreferences } = this.props;
```

```
        /* ... */
    }
}
```

The SearchTextField component

Getting back to our original example, we can leverage the power of `Provider` and `inject()` to get access to `store` (an instance of `BookSearchStore`) at any level in the component tree. `SearchTextField` component makes use of it to become an observer of the `store`:

```
@inject('store')
@observer
export class SearchTextField extends React.Component {
    render() {
        const { store, onChange } = this.props;
        const { term } = store;

        return (
            <Fragment>
                <TextField
                    placeholder={'Search Books...'}
                    InputProps={{
                        startAdornment: (
                            <InputAdornment position="start">
                                <Search />
                            </InputAdornment>
                        ),
                    }}
                    fullWidth={true}
                    value={term}
                    onChange={onChange}
                    onKeyUp={this.onKeyUp}
                />

                <SearchStatus />
            </Fragment>
        );
    }

    onKeyUp = event => {
        if (event.keyCode !== 13) {
            return;
        }

        this.props.onEnter();
```

```
        };
    }
```

SearchTextField observes the term property of store and updates itself when it changes. The change to the term is handled as part of the onChange handler of the TextField. The actual onChange handler is passed as a prop into SearchTextField by the App component. It is inside the App component where we fire the setTerm() action to update the store.term property:

```
@inject('store')
@observer
class App extends React.Component {
    render() {
        const { store } = this.props;

        return (
            <Fragment>
                <Header />

                <Grid container>
                    <Grid item xs={12}>
                        <Paper elevation={2} style={{ padding: '1rem' }}>
                            <SearchTextField
                                onChange={this.updateSearchText}
                                onEnter={store.search}
                            />
                        </Paper>
                    </Grid>

                    <ResultsList style={{ marginTop: '2rem' }} />
                </Grid>
            </Fragment>
        );
    }

    updateSearchText = event => {
        this.props.store.setTerm(event.target.value);
    };
}
```

Now, `SearchTextField` not only handles the updates to the `store.term` observable, but also shows the status of the search operation with the `SearchStatus` component. We include this component right inside `SearchTextField`, but there are no props passed into it. This may seem a little unsettling at first. How in the world is `SearchStatus` going to know about the current `store.status`? Well, this should be obvious once you look at the definition of `SearchStatus`:

```
import React, { Fragment } from 'react';
import { inject, observer } from 'mobx-react';

export const SearchStatus = inject('store')(
    observer(({ store }) => {
        const { status, term } = store;

        return (
            <Fragment>
                {status === 'pending' ? (
                    <LinearProgress variant={'query'} />
                ) : null}

                {status === 'failed' ? (
                    <Typography
                        variant={'subheading'}
                        style={{ color: 'red', marginTop: '1rem' }}
                    >
                        {`Failed to fetch results for "${term}"`}
                    </Typography>
                ) : null}
            </Fragment>
        );
    }),
);
```

Using `inject()`, we get access to the `store` observable, and by wrapping the component with `observer()`, we can react to changes in the observable state (`term`, `status`). Notice the use of the nested calls to `inject('store')(observer( () => {} ))`. The order here is important. You first call `inject()` by requesting the Provider-prop that you want injected. This returns a function that takes a component as input. Here we use `observer()` to create a HOC and pass it to `inject()`.

Since the `SearchStatus` component is pretty much self-contained, `SearchTextField` can simply include it and expect it to work correctly.

When the `store.status` changes, only the virtual-DOM for `SearchStatus` changes, re-rendering just that component. The rest of `SearchTextField` is left unchanged. This rendering efficiency is built into `observer()`, and there is no extra work needed on your part. Internally, `observer()` carefully tracks the observables that are used in `render()` and sets up a `reaction()` to update the component when any of the tracked observables change.

The ResultsList component

With `SearchTextField`, the search action will be invoked when you type some text and hit *Enter*. This changes the observable state, which is partly rendered by `SearchTextField`. However, when the results arrive, the list of books that match the *search-term* are shown by the `ResultsList` component. As expected, it is an *observer-component*, which connects to the `store` observable via `inject()`. But this time, it uses a slightly different approach to connect to `store`:

```
import { inject, observer } from 'mobx-react';

@inject(({ store }) => ({ searchStore: store }))
@observer
export class ResultsList extends React.Component {
    render() {
        const { searchStore, style } = this.props;
        const { isEmpty, results, totalCount, status } = searchStore;

        return (
            <Grid spacing={16} container style={style}>
                {isEmpty && status === 'completed' ? (
                    <Grid item xs={12}>
                        <EmptyResults />
                    </Grid>
                ) : null}

                {!isEmpty && status === 'completed' ? (
                    <Grid item xs={12}>
                        <Typography>
                            Showing <strong>{results.length}</strong>
                            of{' '}
                            {totalCount} results.
                        </Typography>
                        <Divider />
                    </Grid>
                ) : null}
```

```
                {results.map(x => (
                    <Grid item xs={12} key={x.id}>
                        <BookItem book={x} />
                        <Divider />
                    </Grid>
                ))}
            </Grid>
        );
    }
}
```

Notice the use of the @inject decorator that takes in a function to extract
the store observable. This gives you a more type-safe approach rather than using a string
property. You will also see that we renamed store to searchStore in the *extractor-
function*. Thus, the store observable is injected with the name searchStore.

In the render method for the ResultsList, we are doing a few other things that are worth
calling out:

- Checking whether the search results are empty with the isEmpty property. This
  wasn't declared earlier but is really a computed property that checks the length
  of the results array and returns true if it's zero:

```
class BookSearchStore {
    @observable term = 'javascript';
    @observable status = '';
    @observable.shallow results = [];

    @observable totalCount = 0;

    @computed
    get isEmpty() {
        return this.results.length === 0;
    }

    /* ... */
}
```

If the search operation has completed and no results were returned (isEmpty = true), we
show the EmptyResults component.

- If the search completed and we got some results back, we show the counts and
  also a list of results, with each result rendered with the BookItem component.

Thus, our component tree for our app looks as follows:

```
                    ┌─────────────┐
                    │  Provider   │
                    └─────────────┘
                           │
                           ▼
                    ┌─────────────┐
                    │     App     │
                    └─────────────┘
                     ╱           ╲
                    ▼             ▼
        ┌─────────────────┐  ┌─────────────┐
        │ SearchTextField │  │ ResultsList │
        └─────────────────┘  └─────────────┘
                 │                  │        ╲
                 ▼                  ▼         ┌─────────────┐
        ┌─────────────┐  ┌──────────────┐    │  BookItem   │
        │ SearchStatus│  │ EmptyResults │    └─────────────┘
        └─────────────┘  └──────────────┘    ┌─────────────┐
                                             │  BookItem   │
                                             └─────────────┘
                                             ┌─────────────┐
                                             │  BookItem   │
                                             └─────────────┘
```

The **Provider** is literally the provider of the observable state. It relies on the React Context to propagate the `store` observable in the component sub-tree. By decorating components with `inject()` and `observer()`, you can connect to the observable state and react to changes. The **SearchTextField**, **SearchStatus**, and **ResultsList** components rely on `observer()` and `inject()` to give you a reactive-UI.

 With the introduction of `React.createContext()` in React 16.3+, you can create your own `Provider` component if you wish. It might be a little verbose, but it achieves the same purpose—propagating the store across the component sub-tree. Give it a shot, if you feel a little adventurous.

Summary

mobx and mobx-react are two NPM packages that are used extensively to build the Reactive UI. The mobx package provides the API to build the observable state, actions, and reactions. On the other hand, mobx-react gives the binding glue to connect the React components to the observable state and also react to any changes. In our example, we made use of these APIs to build a book search app. When creating your *observer-driven* component tree, make sure to go granular with the use of observers. This way you will react to just the observables you need to render the UI.

The SearchTextField, SearchStatus, and ResultsList components were created with the intent of being granular and reacting to a focused observable surface. This is the recommended way to use MobX with React.

In the next chapter we will dive deeper into MobX, with an exploration of the Observables.

4
Crafting the Observable Tree

Defining the reactive model of your application is usually the first step when working with MobX and React. We know very well that this is all in the realm of the following:

- Observables, which represent the application state
- Actions, which mutate it
- Reactions, which produce side effects by observing the changing observables

When defining the observable state, MobX gives you various tools to carefully control observability. In this chapter, we will explore this side of MobX and take a deeper look at *crafting the observable tree*.

The topics that will be covered in this chapter are the following:

- The shape of data
- Controlling observability with various decorators
- Creating computed properties
- Modeling MobX stores with classes

Technical requirements

You will be required to have JavaScript programming language. Finally, to use the Git repository of this book, the user needs to install Git.

The code files of this chapter can be found on GitHub:
https://github.com/PacktPublishing/MobX-Quick-Start-Guide/tree/master/src/Chapter04

Check out the following video to see the code in action:
http://bit.ly/2uYmln9

The shape of data

The data that we deal with within an application comes in all shapes and sizes. However, these different shapes are fairly limited and can be listed as:

- **Singular values**: These include primitives like numbers, booleans, strings, null, undefined, dates, and so on.
- **Lists**: Your typical list of items where each item is one of a kind. It is generally a good practice to avoid putting items of different data types in the same list. This creates homogenous lists which are easy to reason about.
- **Hierarchy**: Many of the structures we see in UI are hierarchical, like a hierarchy of files and f0lders, parent-child relationships, groups and items, and so on.
- **Composite**: A combination of some or all of the preceding shapes. Most real world data is in this form.

MobX gives us the API to model each of these shapes and we have already seen some examples of this in earlier chapters. However, MobX makes one distinction between singular values and other kinds like arrays and maps. This is reflected in the API as well, where `observable()` can *only* be used to create objects, arrays, and maps. Creating an observable out of a singular value requires us to box it with the `observable.box()` API.

Controlling observability

MobX, by default, applies deep observability on your objects, arrays, and maps. This allows you to see changes happening at any level in the observable tree. Although this a great default to start with, at some point, you will have to pay more attention to limit the observability. Cutting down on the observability also improves performance as there are fewer things to track from the point of view of MobX.

There are two distinct ways in which you can control observability:

- By using the various `@decorators` inside classes
- By using the `decorate()` API

Using @decorators

Decorators are a syntactic feature that allow you to attach behavior to a class and its fields. We have already seen this in `Chapter 3`, *A React App with MobX*, so the following code should be very familiar:

```
class BookSearchStore {
    @observable term = 'javascript';
    @observable status = '';
    @observable.shallow results = [];

    @observable totalCount = 0;
}
```

Using the `@observable` decorator, you can make properties of a class into observables. This is the recommended approach to start modeling your observables. By default, `@observable` applies deep observability, but there are some specialized decorators that give you more control.

> `@observable` is a shorter form or an alias of `@observable.deep`, which is the default decorator. It applies *deep observability* at all levels of objects, arrays, and maps. However, the deep observation stops at places where the object has a *constructor or a prototype*. Such objects are usually instances of classes and are expected to have their own *observable properties*. MobX chooses to skip such objects during deep observation.

Creating shallow observables with @observable.shallow

This decorator prunes the observability to just the first level of the data, also called **one-level-deep** observation, and is particularly useful for observable arrays and maps. In the case of arrays, it will monitor a reference change (for example, assigning a new array) of the array itself, and the addition and removal of items in the array. If you have items in the array that have properties, they would not be considered in the shallow observation. Similarly, for maps, only the addition and removal of keys is considered, along with the reference change of the map itself. Values of the keys in the observable map are left as-is and not considered for observation.

The following snippet shows the application of the `@observable.shallow` decorator.

```
class BookSearchStore {
    @observable term = 'javascript';
    @observable status = '';
    @observable.shallow results = [];

    @observable totalCount = 0;
}
```

We chose to apply this decorator to the `results` property of the `BookSearchStore`. It is clear that that we are not particularly observing the properties of each individual result. In fact, they are read only objects that will never change values, so it makes sense that we prune the observability to just the addition and removal of items, and reference changes in the `results` array. Thus, `observable.shallow` is the right choice here.

 A subtle point to remember here is that the `length` property of the array (`size`, in the case of maps) is also observable. Can you figure out why it is observable?

Creating reference-only observables with @observable.ref

If you are *not* interested in any changes happening inside a data structure (object, array, map) and only in the *change in value*, `@observable.ref` is what you are looking for. It will only monitor reference changes to the observable.

```
import { observable, action } from 'mobx';

class FormData {
    @observable.ref validations = null;

    @observable username = '';
    @observable password = '';

    @action
    validate() {
        const { username, password } = this;
        this.validations = applyValidations({ username, password });
    }
}
```

In the preceding example, the `validations` observable is always assigned a new value. Since we are never modifying the properties of this object, it is better to mark it as `@observable.ref`. This way, we only track reference changes to `validations` and nothing else.

Creating structural observables with @observable.struct

MobX has a built-in behavior to track changes in values and works well for primitives like strings, numbers, booleans, and so on. However, it becomes less than ideal when dealing with *objects*. Every time a new object is assigned to the observable, it will be considered as a change, and reactions will fire. What you really need is a *structural check* where the *properties* of your object are compared instead of the *object reference,* and then decide if there is a change. That is the purpose of `@observable.struct`.

It does a deep comparison based on *property values* rather then relying on the top-level reference. You can think of this as a refinement over the `observable.ref` decorator.

Let's look at the following code, where we create an `@observable.struct` for the `location` property:

```
class Sphere {
    @observable.struct location = { x: 0, y: 0 };

    constructor() {
        autorun(() => {
            console.log(
                `Current location: (${this.location.x},
${this.location.y})`,
            );
        });
    }

    @action
    moveTo(x, y) {
        this.location = { x, y };
    }
}

let x = new Sphere();

x.moveTo(0, 0);
x.moveTo(20, 30);
```

```
// Prints
Current location: (0, 0)
Current location: (20, 30)
```

Notice that `autorun()` fires once immediately and then does not react to the next location (`{ x: 0, y: 0 }`). Since the structural value is the same (`0, 0`), it is not treated as a change and hence no notifications are fired. It's only when we set the location to a different (`x, y`) value that `autorun()` is triggered.

We can now represent the level of observability of the decorators, as in the following diagram. `@observable` (in this case, `@observable.deep`) is the most powerful, followed by `@observable.shallow`, `@observable.ref`, and finally `@observable.struct`. As you get more fine-grained with the observable decorators, you can prune the surface area to track in the observable tree. This is shown with the orange-colored shapes. The more observables there are, the greater the tracking area is for MobX:

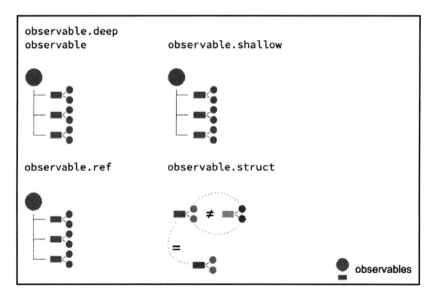

Using the decorate() API

The use of `@decorators` is definitely very convenient and readable, but it does require some setup with Babel (using *babel-plugin-transform-decorators-legacy*) or turning on the `experimentalDecorators` flag in the compiler options for TypeScript. With version 4, MobX introduced an *ES5* API for decorating the observable properties of an object or class.

Using the `decorate()` API, you can selectively target properties and specify the observability. The following code snippet should make this clear:

```
import { action, computed, decorate, observable } from 'mobx';

class BookSearchStore {
 term = 'javascript';
 status = '';
 results = [];

 totalCount = 0;

 get isEmpty() {
 return this.results.length === 0;
 }

 setTerm(value) {
 this.term = value;
 }

 async search() {}
}

decorate(BookSearchStore, {
 term: observable,
 status: observable,
 results: observable.shallow,
 totalCount: observable,

 isEmpty: computed,
 setTerm: action.bound,
 search: action.bound,
});

decorate(target, decorator-object)
```

The `target` can be an object prototype or a class type. The second argument is an object containing the target properties that you want to decorate.

In the preceding example, notice the way that we are applying the decorators to the class type. From a developer standpoint, it feels natural to use them when you don't have the syntax support of `@decorators`. In fact, the `decorate()` API can also be used for other kinds of decorators such as `action`, `action.bound`, and `computed`.

Decorating with observable()

The `decorate()` style of the API also works when declaring observables using the `observable()` API.

`observable(properties, decorators, options)`:Its arguments are as follows:

- `properties`: Declare the properties of the observable object
- `decorators`: An object defining the decorators for the properties
- `options`: Options for setting default observability and a debug-friendly name (`{ deep: false|true, name: string }`)

The second argument to `observable()` is where you specify the decorators for various properties in your object. This works exactly like the `decorate()` call, as can be seen in the following code snippet:

```
import { action, computed, observable } from 'mobx';

const cart = observable(
    {
        items: [],
        modified: new Date(),
        get hasItems() {
            return this.items.length > 0;
        },
        addItem(name, quantity) {
            /* ... */
        },
        removeItem(name) {
            /* ... */
        },
    },
    {
        items: observable.shallow,
        modified: observable,

        hasItems: computed,
        addItem: action.bound,
        removeItem: action.bound,
    },
);
```

In the second argument, we have applied the various decorators to control the *observability*, apply *actions*, and mark *computed properties*.

When using the `observable()` API, it is not required to mark the computed properties explicitly. MobX will convert any `getter` property of the passed in object into a computed property.

Similarly, for the `modified` property, there is actually no need to decorate since `observable()` by default makes everything deeply observable. We only have to specify the properties that need a different treatment. In other words, only specify decorators for the exceptional properties.

Extending the observability

When modeling the client state, it is best to pre-define the observability we need in our reactive system. This bakes in all the constraints and scope of the observable data in your domain. However, the real world is always unforgiving and there will be times where you need runtime abilities to extend the observability. This is where the `extendObservable()` API comes in. It allows you to mix in additional properties at runtime and make them observable as well.

In the following example, we are extending the observability of the `cart` for festive offers:

```
import { observable, action, extendObservable } from 'mobx';

const cart = observable({
    /* ... */
});

function applyFestiveOffer(cart) {
    extendObservable(
        cart,
        {
            coupons: ['OFF50FORU'],
            get hasCoupons() {
                return this.coupons && this.coupons.length > 0;
            },
            addCoupon(coupon) {
                this.coupons.push(coupon);
            },
        },
        {
            coupons: observable.shallow,
            addCoupon: action,
```

```
        },
    );
}
```

```
extendObservable(target, object, decorators)
```

The *first* argument to `extendObservable()` is the target object that we want to extend. The second argument is the list of observable properties and actions that will be mixed into the target object. The third argument is the list of decorators that will be applied to the properties.

In the preceding example, we want to add more observables to the **cart** for tracking festive offers. This can only be done at runtime based on an active festive season. The `applyFestiveOffers()` function is called when that condition is met.

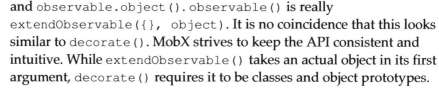

`extendObservable()` is in fact the superset of `observable()`, and `observable.object().observable()` is really `extendObservable({}, object)`. It is no coincidence that this looks similar to `decorate()`. MobX strives to keep the API consistent and intuitive. While `extendObservable()` takes an actual object in its first argument, `decorate()` requires it to be classes and object prototypes.

[Fun Fact] Before the introduction of `decorate()`, `extendObservable()` was used to extend `this` inside the *class constructor*: `extendObservable(this, { })`. Of course, now the recommended approach is to use `decorate()`, which can be applied directly on a class or object prototype.

One point to ponder on is that an *observable Map* could also be used to add observable properties on the fly. However, they can only be *state carrying* properties and not *actions* or *computed-properties*. When you want to dynamically add *actions* and *computed properties* as well, go for `extendObservable()`.

Derived state with @computed

One of the core philosophies of MobX is that the observable state should be as minimal as possible. Everything else should be *derived* via computed properties. This perspective makes sense when we talk about state management in UI. The UI is always nuanced on the same observable state and needs different views of the state depending on the context and task. This means that there are many possibilities for deriving a view-centric state (or representation) within the same UI.

An example of such a view-centric state is a table view and a chart view of the same list of observables. Both are operating on the same state but need different representations to satisfy the UI (the view) needs. Such representations are prime candidates for state derivations. MobX recognizes this core requirement and provides *computed properties*, which are specialized observables that derive their value from other dependent observables.

Computed properties are very efficient and cache the computation. Although the computed property is re-evaluated whenever the dependent observables change, no notifications are fired if the new value matches the previously cached value. Additionally, computed properties also get garbage collected if there are no more observers of the computed property. This automatic cleanup also adds to the efficiency. *Caching* and *automatic clean-up* are the main reasons why MobX recommends liberal usage of computed properties.

Using computed properties, we can create separate observables as needed by the UI. As your application grows in size, you will possibly need more derivations that depend on the core state. These derivations (computed properties) can be mixed in using `extendObservable()`, as and when needed.

MobX offers three different ways in which you can create computed properties: using the `@computed` decorator, the `decorate()` API, or using the `computed()` function. These can be seen in the following code snippet:

```
import { observable, computed, decorate } from 'mobx';

// 1. Using @computed
class Cart {
    @observable.shallow items = [];

    @computed
    get hasItems() {
        return this.items.length > 0;
    }
}
```

```
// 2. Using decorate()
class Cart2 {
    items = [];

    get hasItems() {
        return this.items.length > 0;
    }
}
decorate(Cart2, {
    items: observable.shallow,
    hasItems: computed,
});

// 3. Using computed()
const cart = new Cart();

const isCartEmpty = computed(() => {
    return cart.items.length === 0;
});

console.log(isCartEmpty.get());

const disposer = isCartEmpty.observe(change =>
console.log(change.newValue));
```

Using the `computed()` function directly has the feel of working with boxed observables. You have to use the `get()` method on the returned computed function to retrieve the value.

You also have the option of using the `observe()` method of the `computed()` function. By attaching an observer, you can get the changed value. This technique can also be used to handle side effects or reactions.

Both of these APIs can be seen in the preceding code snippet. This usage is not very common, but can be leveraged when dealing with boxed observables directly.

Structural equality

If the return value of a computed property is a primitive, it is easy to know when there is a new value. MobX compares the previous value of the computed property with the newly evaluated value and then fires notifications if they differ. Thus, value comparisons become important to ensure notifications are fired only on a *real change*.

For objects, this is not straightforward. The default comparison is done based on reference checks (using the === operator). This treats the objects as being different even though the values within them are exactly the same.

In the following example, the metrics computed property generates a new object every time the start or end properties change. Since the autorun (defined in the constructor) depends on metrics, it runs the side effect every time metrics changes:

```
import { observable, computed, action, autorun } from 'mobx';

class DailyPrice {
    @observable start = 0;
    @observable end = 0;

    @computed
    get metrics() {
        const { start, end } = this;
        return {
            delta: end - start,
        };
    }

    @action
    update(start, end) {
        this.start = start;
        this.end = end;
    }

    constructor() {
        autorun(() => {
            const { delta } = this.metrics;
            console.log(`Price Delta = ${delta}`);
        });
    }
}

const price = new DailyPrice();

// Changing start and end, but metrics don't change
price.update(0, 10);
price.update(10, 20);
price.update(20, 30);
```

However, notice that metrics doesn't really change, even though
the start and end properties are changing. This can be seen with the *autorun* side effect,
which keeps printing the same delta value. This happens because the metrics computed
property is returning a new object on each evaluation:

```
Price Delta = 0;
Price Delta = 10;
Price Delta = 10;
Price Delta = 10;
```

The way to fix this is to use the @computed.struct decorator, which does a deep
comparison of the object structure. This ensures that no notifications are fired when a re-
evaluation of the metrics property gives back the same structure.

This is one way to safeguard a costly reaction that depends on such a computed observable.
Decorate it with computed.struct to ensure only a real change in the object structure is
considered for notification. Conceptually, it is very similar to
the observable.struct decorator that we saw in the previous section of this chapter:

```
class DailyPrice {
    @observable start = 0;
    @observable end = 0;

    @computed.struct
    get metrics() {
        const { start, end } = this;
        return {
            delta: end - start,
        };
    }
    // ...
}
```

In practice, it is rare to use the computed.struct observable. The computed value only
changes when the dependent observables change. When any of the dependent observables
change, a new, computed value has to be created, and in most real world apps, it is
different most of the time. Thus, you don't really need to decorate with computed.struct,
since most computed values will be very different from each other in successive
evaluations.

Modeling the stores

It can seem like a daunting task when you start to model the client state for your React Application with MobX. An idea that can help you on this journey is the simple realization that *your application is just a collection of features*, composed together to form a cohesive unit. By starting with the simplest feature, you can string the rest of the app together, one feature at a time.

This style of thinking guides you to model your feature-level-stores first. The app-level-store (also called the Root Store) is just a composition of these feature stores with a shared communication channel. In the MobX world, you start with a *class* to describe the feature store. Depending on the complexity, you can break the feature store into many sub stores. The feature store acts as the coordinator of all the sub stores. This is the classic *divide and conquer* approach to modeling software:

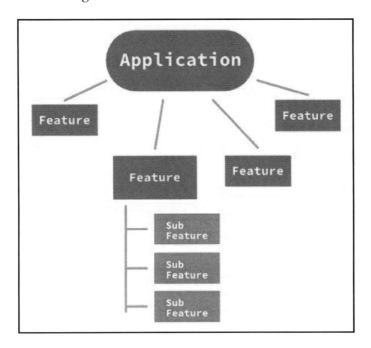

Let's take an example to illustrate this approach to modeling the reactive client state. In the *book-search* app that we built in the previous section, we want to add the ability to create wishlists. A wishlist can contain items that you would like to purchase in the future. You should be able to create as many wishlists as you want. Let's model the wishlist feature with MobX. We will not worry about the React side of things and instead just focus on using MobX to model the client state.

The Wishlist feature

This adds the ability to create wishlists. A wishlist has a name and contains a list of items to be purchased in the future. One can create as many wishlists as needed. A wishlist item has the title of the item and a flag to track if it is purchased.

The first step in modeling with MobX is to identify the *observable state* and the *actions* that can mutate it. We are not going to worry about *reactions* (or *observers*) as of now.

Observable state

We will start with a *class*, WishListStore, to track all the details of the wishlist feature. This is our *feature-level-store* that contains the observable state for the entire feature. Based on the description we saw earlier, let's distill the core observable state:

- An array of wishlists, where each item is an instance of a WishList class
- The WishList has a *name* and contains an array of WishListItem instances
- Each WishListItem has a *title* and a boolean *purchased* property

An interesting thing to note here is that we have extracted some vocabulary from the earlier description. This includes WishListStore, WishList, and WishListItem, which form the backbone of our feature. Identifying this vocabulary is the hard part and can take a few iterations to get to the right terms. It's no wonder that *naming things* is classified as one of the two hard problems in Computer Science!

In code, we can now capture this observable state as follows:

```
import { observable } from 'mobx';

class WishListStore {
    @observable.shallow lists = [];
}

class WishList {
    @observable name = '';
    @observable.shallow items = [];
}

class WishListItem {
    @observable title = '';
    @observable purchased = false;
}
```

```
const store = new WishListStore();
```

Notice the use of the `observable.shallow` decorator for arrays. We don't need deep observation for them. The individual items (`WishListItem`) have their own observable properties. The wishlist feature is represented by the singleton instance of the `WishListStore` (`store`). Since we will be creating instances of `WishList` and `WishListItem`, we can add constructor functions to make this easier:

```
class WishList {
    @observable name = '';
    @observable.shallow items = [];

    constructor(name) {
        this.name = name;
    }
}

class WishListItem {
    @observable title = '';
    @observable purchased = false;

    constructor(title) {
        this.title = title;
    }
}
```

Derived state

Now that the core observable state has been established, we can give some consideration to the derived state. Derived state (derivations) are computed properties that depend on other observables. It is helpful to think of the derivations in the context of how the core observable state is consumed.

One common use case when you have arrays is to think of the empty state. There is usually some visual indication that the list is empty. Rather than testing the `array.length`, which is quite low-level, it is better to expose a computed property called `isEmpty`. Such computed properties focus on the *semantics* of our store rather than dealing directly with the core observables:

```
class WishListStore {
    @observable.shallow lists = [];

    @computed
    get isEmpty() {
```

```
            return this.lists.length === 0;
    }
}

class WishList {
    @observable name = '';
    @observable.shallow items = [];

    @computed
    get isEmpty() {
        return this.items.length === 0;
    }

    /* ... */
}
```

Similarly, if we want to know the purchased items from the `WishList`, there is no need to define any new observable state. It can be derived from the `items` by filtering the `purchased` property. That is the definition for the `purchasedItems` *computed property*. I'll leave it as an exercise for the reader to define this computed property.

You should always think of the *observable state* as a combination of a minimal *core state* and a *derived state*. Think of the following equation to ensure that you are not putting too much into your core state. What can be derived should always lie in the *derived state*:

$$ObservableState = CoreState + DerivedState$$

In real-world apps, it is quite possible that a property being tracked in one store may move to another due to refactoring. For example, the `purchased` property of a `WishListItem` could be tracked by a separate store (for example, `ShoppingCartStore`). In such a case, the `WishListItem` can make it a *computed property* and depend on the external store to keep track of it. Doing so does not change anything on the UI since the way you read `purchased` still stays the same. Also, MobX makes it simple to keep the `purchased` property always up-to-date because of the implicit dependency created via the computed property.

Actions

Once the observable state is identified, it is natural to include the *actions* that can mutate it. These are the operations which will be invoked by the user, and exposed by the React interface. In the case of the wishlist feature, this includes:

- Creating a new WishList
- Deleting a wishlist
- Renaming a wishlist
- Adding items (WishListItem) to a wishlist
- Removing items from a wishlist

Actions that add or remove wishlists go into the top-level, WishListStore, while actions concerning items in a wishlist will be placed in the WishList class. The renaming of a wishlist can also go into the WishList class:

```
import { observable, action } from 'mobx';

class WishListStore {
    @observable.shallow lists = [];

    /* ... */

    @action
    addWishList(name) {
        this.lists.push(new WishList(name));
    }

    @action
    removeWishList(list) {
        this.lists.remove(list);
    }
}

class WishList {
    @observable name = '';
    @observable.shallow items = [];

    /* ... */

    @action
    renameWishList(newName) {
        this.name = newName;
    }
```

```
@action
addItem(title) {
    this.items.push(new WishListItem(title));
}

@action
removeItem(item) {
    this.items.remove(item);
}
}
```

 MobX gives a convenient API on *observable arrays* to remove items. Using the `remove()` method, you can remove items that match by value or reference. The method returns *true* if the item was found and removed.

Summary

Once you make the broad cuts on the observable state, it is time to tailor it further with the observable decorators. This gives you better control of the observability and improves the performance of the MobX reactivity system. We have seen two different ways of doing this: one with the `@decorator` syntax and the other using the `decorate()` API.

It is also possible to add new *observable properties* on the fly with `extendObservable()`. In fact, you can even add new *actions* and *computed properties* with `extendObservable()`.

Observable State = Core State + Derived State

The *core state* and the *derived state* are two aspects of the *observable state* in MobX. This is easy to model with classes and decorators, as shown in the preceding sections. Once you identify the vocabulary of your feature, they become the class names that encapsulate the *observable state*. To handle the complexity of the feature, you can break it into smaller classes and compose them in the *feature store*. These *feature stores* are then composed in the top-level *root store*.

Now that we have a deeper understanding of defining and crafting the *observables,* it's time we look at the other pillars of MobX: *actions* and *reactions*. That is where we are heading with the next chapter.

5
Derivations, Actions, and Reactions

Now that the MobX foundations have been laid with the three pillars of *observables*, *actions*, and *reactions*, it's time we go deeper and understand the finer aspects. In this chapter, we will explore the core philosophies and nuances of the MobX API, as well as some special APIs to simplify asynchronous programming in MobX.

The topics covered in this chapter include:

- Computed properties (also known as derivations) and their various options
- Actions, with special focus on async actions
- Reactions and the rules governing when MobX reacts

Technical requirements

You will be required to have Node.js installed on a system. Finally, to use the Git repository of this book, the user needs to install Git.

The code files of this chapter can be found on GitHub:
`https://github.com/PacktPublishing/MobX-Quick-Start-Guide/tree/master/src/Chapter05`

Check out the following video to see the code in action:
`http://bit.ly/2mAvXk9`

Derivations (computed properties)

Derivation is a term that is used quite frequently in the MobX parlance. It is given special emphasis in client-state modeling. As we saw in the previous chapter, the observable state can be determined by the combination of the *core-mutable-state* and a *derived-read-only-state*:

Observable State = (Core-mutable-State) + (Derived-readonly-State)

It is essential to keep the core state as lean as possible. This is the part that is expected to stay stable and grow slowly during the lifetime of the application. It is only the core state that is actually mutable and the *actions* always mutate only the *core state*. The derived state depends on the core state and is kept up-to-date by the MobX reactivity system. We know that *computed properties* act as the derived state in MobX. They can depend not only on the *core state* but also on other derived states, creating a dependency tree that is kept alive by MobX:

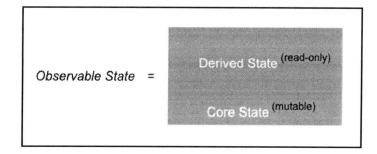

A key characteristic of the derived state is that it is *read only*. Its job is to generate a *computed value* (using the *core state*) but never mutate the *core state*. MobX is smart to cache these computed values and not perform any unnecessary computation. It also does efficient clean-ups when there are no observers of the *computed values*. It is highly recommended to leverage the computed properties as much as possible and not worry about the performance impact.

Let's take an example where you can have a minimal core state and a derived state for satisfying the UI needs. Consider the humble `Todo`, `TodoList`, and `TodoManager`. You can probably guess what these classes do. They form the observable state of a *Todos* application:

```
import { computed, decorate, observable, autorun, action } from 'mobx';

class Todo {
    @observable title = '';
    @observable done = false;
```

```
        constructor(title) {
            this.title = title;
        }
    }

class TodoList {
    @observable.shallow todos = [];

    @computed
    get pendingTodos() {
        return this.todos.filter(x => x.done === false);
    }

    @computed
    get completedTodos() {
        return this.todos.filter(x => x.done);
    }

    @computed
    get pendingTodosDescription() {
        const count = this.pendingTodos.length;
        return `${count} ${count === 1 ? 'todo' : 'todos'} remaining`;
    }

    @action
    addTodo(title) {
        const todo = new Todo(title);
        this.todos.push(todo);
    }
}

class TodoManager {
    list = null;

    @observable filter = 'all'; // all, pending, completed
    @observable title = ''; // user-editable title when creating a new
    todo

    constructor(list) {
        this.list = list;

        autorun(() => {
            console.log(this.list.pendingTodos.length);
        });
    }

    @computed
    get visibleTodos() {
```

```
        switch (this.filter) {
            case 'pending':
                return this.list.pendingTodos;
            case 'completed':
                return this.list.completedTodos;
            default:
                return this.list.todos;
        }
    }
}
```

As you can see from the preceding code, the core state is defined by the properties marked with @observable. They are the mutable properties of these classes. For a *Todos* app, the core state is primarily the list of Todo items.

The derived state, which is mostly to take care of the filtering needs of the UI, includes the properties marked with @computed. Of particular interest is the TodoList class, which only has one @observable: an array of todos. Rest is the derived state consisting of the pendingTodos, pendingTodosDescription, and completedTodos, all marked by @computed.

By keeping a lean core state, we can produce many variations of the derived state, as needed by the UI. Such a derived state could also help in keeping the semantic model clean and simple. This also gives you a chance to *enforce the vocabulary of the domain* rather than exposing the raw core state directly.

Is it a side effect?

In Chapter 1, *Introduction to State Management*, we talked about the role of side effects. These are the reactive aspects of the application that produce *external effects* based on changes in state (also known as data). If we now look at *computed properties* through the lens of side effects, you can find it very similar to the reactions in MobX. After all, a reaction in MobX looks at observables and produces side effects. This is what a computed-property does too! It depends on observables and produces an observable-value as side effect. So, shouldn't *computed properties* be considered as side effects?

Very sound argument indeed. It can appear as a side effect from the way it is derived, but the fact that it generates an *observable-value* brings it back into the world of *client-state* rather than becoming an external effect. Computed properties are, in fact, data for the UI and other state-management aspects. Unlike the side effect-causing functions of MobX, such as autorun(), reaction(), and when(), computed properties don't cause any *external* side effects and stay within the confines of the client-state.

Another clear distinction between MobX reactions and computed properties is that there is an implicit expectation that *computed properties will give back a value,* whereas reactions are *fire-and-forget* with no expectation of getting back a value. Also, with computed properties the re-evaluation (the *side effect* part of a computed-property) can stop as soon as there are no more observers. However, with reactions, it is not always clear when to stop them. For example, it is not always clear when logging or a network request should be stopped.

So, let's rest the case by saying that *computed properties* are only a *partial side effect* and not the full-on, fire-and-forget reactions of MobX.

There's more to computed()

So far, we have looked at the use of the `@computed` decorator along with `@computed.struct`, where structural equality was crucial. There is of course more to the `computed` function, which also takes several options for a fine-grained customization. These options are available when used in the `decorate()` function, the `@computed` decorator, or when creating *boxed-computed observables*.

In the following snippet, we see the usage in the `decorate()` function, which is more common:

```
class TodoList {
    @observable.shallow todos = [];
    get pendingTodos() {
        return this.todos.filter(x => x.done === false);
    }

    get completedTodos() {
        return this.todos.filter(x => x.done);
    }

    @action
    addTodo(title) {
        const todo = new Todo(title);
        this.todos.push(todo);
    }
}

decorate(TodoList, {
    pendingTodos: computed({ name: 'pending-todos', /* other options */ }),
});
```

Options for `computed()` can be passed as an *object-argument* with several properties:

- `name`: This is useful when combined with MobX DevTools (part of the ***mobx-react-devtools*** NPM package). The name specified here is used in logs and also when introspecting the *observables* of a rendered React component.
- `context`: The value of *"this"* inside the computed function. In general, you don't need to specify as it will default to the decorated instance.
- `set`: A *computed-property* is most often used as a *getter*. But, you could supply a setter too. This is not to replace the value of the computed property, but rather acts as an *inverse*. Consider the following example, where the setter for `fullName` is splitting it into `firstName` and `lastName`:

```
class Contact {
    @observable firstName = '';
    @observable lastName = '';

    get fullName() {
        return `${this.firstName} ${this.lastName}`;
    }

}

decorate(Contact, {
    fullName: computed({
        // extract firstName and lastName
        set: function(value) {
            const [firstName, lastName] = value.split(' ');

            this.firstName = firstName;
            this.last = lastName;
        },
    }),
});
```

To do the same inside the class, without `decorate()`, you just add a setter, as seen in the following code:

```
class Contact {
    @observable firstName = '';
    @observable lastName = '';

    @computed
    get fullName() {
        return `${this.firstName} ${this.lastName}`;
    }
```

```
    set fullName(value) {
        const [firstName, lastName] = value.split(' ');

        this.firstName = firstName;
        this.lastName = lastName;
    }
}

const c = new Contact();

c.firstName = 'Pavan';
c.lastName = 'Podila';

console.log(c.fullName); // Prints: Pavan Podila

c.fullName = 'Michel Weststrate';
console.log(c.firstName, c.lastName); // Prints: Michel Weststrate
```

- keepAlive: There are times when you need a computed value to be always available, even when there are no tracking observers. This option keeps the computed value *hot* and always updated. One caution with this option is that the computed value will *always be cached* and you may want to think more deeply for possible memory leaks and expensive computations. Objects with computed properties with { keepAlive: true } can only be garbage-collected when all of their dependent observables are garbage-collected. So, use this option with care.

- requiresReaction: This is a property meant to safeguard against *expensive computations running more often than expected*. The default is set to false, which means even without an observer (also known as reaction) it will be evaluated the first time. When set to true, it does not perform the computation if there are no observers. Instead, it throws an error informing you of the need for an observer. It is possible to change the global behavior by calling configure({ computedRequiresReaction: Boolean }).

- equals: This sets the equality checker for the computed property. The equality check determines if a notification needs to be fired to inform all observers (also known as reactions). As we know, only when the *newly-computed value* is different from the *previously-cached-value* will a notification be fired. The default is comparer.identity, which does a === check. In other words, a value and a reference check. The other kind of equality check is with comparer.structural, which performs a deep comparison of the values to determine if they are equal. Conceptually, it is similar to an observable.struct decorator. This is also the comparer used for the computed.struct decorator:

```
import { observable, computed, decorate, comparer } from 'mobx';

class Contact {
    @observable firstName = '';
    @observable lastName = '';

    get fullName() {
        return `${this.firstName} ${this.lastName}`;
    }

}

decorate(Contact, {
    fullName: computed({
        set: function(value) {
            const [firstName, lastName] = value.split(' ');

            this.firstName = firstName;
            this.last = lastName;
        },
        equals: comparer.identity,
    }),

});
```

Error handling inside computed

Computed properties have the special ability to recover from errors thrown during computation. Rather than bailing out immediately, they catch and hold on to the error. It is only when you try to read from a *computed-property*, that it will rethrow the error. This gives you the chance to recover by resetting some state and getting back to some default state.

The following example is straight from the MobX docs, and aptly demonstrates the error recovery:

```
import { observable, computed } from 'mobx';

const x = observable.box(3);
const y = observable.box(1);

const divided = computed(() => {
    if (y.get() === 0) {
        throw new Error('Division by zero');
    }

    return x.get() / y.get();
});

divided.get(); // returns 3

y.set(0); // OK

try {
    divided.get(); // Throws: Division by zero
        } catch (ex) {
    // Recover to a safe state
    y.set(2);
}

divided.get(); // Recovered; Returns 1.5
```

Actions

Actions are the way to mutate the core state of your application. In fact, MobX strongly recommends that you always use actions and never do any mutations outside of an action. It even goes to the extent of enforcing this requirement across your app if you `configure` MobX with: `{ enforceActions: true }`:

```
import { configure } from 'mobx';

configure({ enforceActions: true });
```

Let the preceding lines of code be the starting point of your *MobX-driven* React app. It's obvious that there are some benefits to using actions for all state-mutation. But so far, it hasn't been very clear. Let's drill a little deeper to uncover these hidden benefits.

`configure({ enforceActions: true })` isn't the only option available for guarding state-mutation. There is a stricter form with `{ enforceActions: 'strict' }`. The difference is subtle but worth calling out. When set to `true`, you are still allowed to make stray mutations outside of an action, **if** there are *no observers* tracking the mutating observable. This may seem like a slip on the part of MobX. However, it is OK to allow this because there are no side effects happening yet, since there are no observers. It won't cause any harm to the consistency of the MobX reactivity system. It's like the old saying, *If a tree falls in the forest and no one is around, does it make a sound?* Maybe too philosophical, but the gist is: without observers, you have no-one tracking observables and causing side effects, so you can safely apply the mutation.

But, if you do want to go the purist route, you can use `{ enforceActions: 'strict' }` and call foul even in cases where there are no observers. It's really a personal choice here.

Why an action?

When an observable is changed, MobX immediately fires a notification informing every observer of the change. So, if you happen to change 10 observables, 10 notifications will be sent out. At times, this is just excessive. You don't want a noisy system that notifies too eagerly. It is better to batch up the notifications and send them in one shot instead. It saves on CPU cycles, keeps your battery on your mobile device happy, and in general leads to a balanced, healthier app.

That is exactly what an `action()` achieves when you put all your mutations inside it. It wraps the mutating-function with `untracked()` and `transaction()`, two special-purpose, low-level utilities inside MobX. `untracked()` prevents tracking of observables (also known as creation of new *observable-observer* relationships) inside the mutating function; whereas `transaction()` batches the notifications, coerces notifications on the same observable, and then dispatches the minimal set of notifications at the end of *action*.

There is one more core utility function that is used by actions, which is `allowStateChanges(true)`. This ensures state changes do happen on the observables and they get their new values. The combination of *untracked, transaction*, and *allowStateChanges* is what makes up an action:

action = untracked(transaction(allowStateChanges(true, <mutating-function>)))

This combination has the following much-intended effects:

- Reducing excessive notifications
- Improving efficiency by batching up a minimal set of notifications
- Minimizing executions of *side effects*, for observables that change several times in an *action*

In fact, actions can be nested within each other, which ensures the notifications only go out after the *outermost action* has finished executing.

Actions also help bring out the semantics of the domain and enable your app to become more declarative. By wrapping the details of how the observables are mutated, you give a *distinct name* to the operation that changes state. This emphasizes the *vocabulary* of your domain and codifies it as part of your *state-management*. This is a nod to the principles of *Domain-Driven Design* that brings the ubiquitous language (the terms of your domain) into the client-side code.

Actions help in bridging the gap between the vocabulary of your domain and names used in the actual code. Besides the efficiency benefits, you also get the semantic benefits that keep the code more readable.

We saw earlier, in the *Derivations (computed properties)* section, that you can also have setters. These setters are automatically wrapped by an `action()` by MobX. A setter for a computed-property is not really changing the computed-property directly. Instead, it is the inverse that mutates the dependent observables that make up the computed-property. Since we are mutating observables, it makes sense to wrap them in an action. MobX is smart enough to do this for you.

Async actions

Asynchronous programming is pervasive in JavaScript, and MobX fully embraces that idea without adding too much ceremony. Here is a small snippet showing some async code interspersed with MobX state mutation:

```
class ShoppingCart {
    @observable asyncState = '';

    @observable.shallow items = [];

    @action
    async submit() {
        this.asyncState = 'pending';
        try {
            const response = await this.purchaseItems(this.items);

            this.asyncState = 'completed'; // modified outside of
            action
        } catch (ex) {
            console.error(ex);
            this.asyncState = 'failed'; // modified outside of action
        }
    }

    purchaseItems(items) {
        /* ... */
        return Promise.resolve({});
    }
}
```

Looks normal, like any other async code. This is exactly the point. By default, MobX simply steps aside and lets you mutate the observables as expected. However, if you configure MobX to { enforceActions: 'strict' }, you get a warm **red** welcome on the console:

```
Unhandled Rejection (Error): [mobx] Since strict-mode is enabled, changing
observed observable values outside actions is not allowed. Please wrap the
code in an `action` if this change is intended. Tried to modify:
ShoppingCart@14.asyncState
```

What's wrong here, you may ask? It has to do with our use of async-await operators. You see, the code that follows the await is *not executed* synchronously. It executes *after* the await promise fulfills. Now, the action() decorator can only guard code that is executed synchronously within its block. Code that is run asynchronously is not considered, and thus runs outside the action(). Hence, the code following await is not part of action anymore, causing MobX to complain.

Wrapping with runInAction()

The way to circumvent this problem is to use a utility function provided by MobX, called runInAction(). This is a handy function that takes in a *mutating-function* and executes it inside an action(). In the following code, you can see the use of runInAction() to wrap the mutations:

```
import { action, observable, configure, runInAction } from 'mobx';

configure({ enforceActions: 'strict' });

class ShoppingCart {
    @observable asyncState = '';

    @observable.shallow items = [];

    @action
    async submit() {
        this.asyncState = 'pending';
        try {
            const response = await this.purchaseItems(this.items);

            runInAction(() => {
                this.asyncState = 'completed';
            });
        } catch (ex) {
            console.error(ex);

            runInAction(() => {
                this.asyncState = 'failed';
            });
        }
    }

    purchaseItems(items) {
        /* ... */
        return Promise.resolve({});
    }
}

const cart = new ShoppingCart();

cart.submit();
```

Note that we have applied runInAction() to the code following await, both in the *try-block* and in the *catch-block*.

runInAction(fn) is just a convenience utility that is equivalent to action(fn)().

Although *async-await* provides a beautiful, concise syntax to write async code, beware of the parts of code that are not synchronous. The co-location of the code within the action() block can be misleading. At runtime, not all statements execute synchronously. The code that follows await is always run async, after the *awaited-promise* fulfills. Wrapping the parts that are async with runInAction() gives us back the benefits of the action() decorator. Now, MobX has no more complaints when you configure ({ enforceActions: 'strict' }).

flow()

In the previous, simple example, we only had to wrap two segments of the code in runInAction(). That was quite straightforward and did not involve too much effort. However, there will be cases where you will have multiple await statements within a function. Consider the login() method shown next, which performs an action involving multiple *awaits*:

```
import { observable, action } from 'mobx';

class AuthStore {
    @observable loginState = '';

    @action.bound
    async login(username, password) {
        this.loginState = 'pending';

        await this.initializeEnvironment();

        this.loginState = 'initialized';

        await this.serverLogin(username, password);

        this.loginState = 'completed';

        await this.sendAnalytics();

        this.loginState = 'reported';
    }

    async initializeEnvironment() {}
```

```
    async serverLogin(username, password) {}

    async sendAnalytics() {}
}
```

Wrapping the state-mutations in `runInAction()` after each `await` can quickly turn cumbersome. You can even forget wrapping some parts if there are more conditionals involved or if the mutations are spread across multiple functions. What if there was a way to automatically wrap the asynchronous parts of the code in `action()`?

MobX provides a solution for this use-case too. There is a utility function called `flow()` that takes a *generator-function* as input. Instead of `await`, you use the `yield` operator instead. Conceptually, it is very similar to the *async-await* kind of code, but uses a *generator function* with `yield` statements to achieve the same effect. Let's rewrite the code from the previous example, using the `flow()` utility:

```
import { observable, action, flow, configure } from 'mobx';

configure({ enforceActions: 'strict' });

class AuthStore {
    @observable loginState = '';

    login = flow(function*(username, password) {
        this.loginState = 'pending';

        yield this.initializeEnvironment();

        this.loginState = 'initialized';

        yield this.serverLogin(username, password);

        this.loginState = 'completed';

        yield this.sendAnalytics();

        this.loginState = 'reported';

        yield this.delay(3000);
    });

}

new AuthStore().login();
```

Notice the use of the generator `function*()` instead of the regular function, which is passed as argument to `flow()`. Structurally, it is no different than the *async-await* style of code, but has the added benefit of automatically wrapping the parts of code following a `yield` with an `action()`. With `flow()`, you are back to being more declarative with your async code.

There is yet another benefit that `flow()` gives you. It is the ability to *cancel execution of the async code*.

The return value of `flow()` is a function that you can invoke to execute the async code. This is the `login` method of the `AuthStore`, in the preceding example. When you call `new AuthStore().login()`, you get back a promise that has been enhanced by MobX with the `cancel()` method:

```
const promise = new AuthStore().login2();
promise.cancel(); // prematurely cancel the async code
```

This is useful for canceling a long-running operation by giving user-level control.

Reactions

Observables and actions keep things within the confines of the MobX reactivity system. Actions mutate the observables and, through the power of notifications, the rest of the MobX system aligns to the mutation to keep the state consistent. To start making a change outside of this MobX system, you need *reactions*. It is the bridge to the outside world that informs the *state-changes* happening within the MobX world.

Consider reactions to be the reactive-bridge-crossing between MobX and the outside world. These are also the side effect producers of your application.

We know that reactions come in three flavors: `autorun`, `reaction`, and `when`. These three flavors have distinct characteristics that tackle the various scenarios within your app.

When determining which one to pick, you can apply this simple decision-making process:

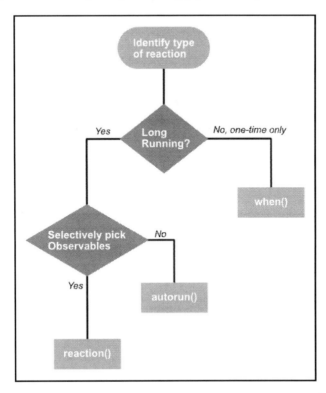

Each of the reactions give you back a *disposer-function*, which can be used to prematurely dispose the reaction thus:

```
import { autorun, reaction, when } from 'mobx';

const disposer1 = autorun(() => {
    /* effect function */
});

const disposer2 = reaction(
    () => {
        /* tracking function returning data */
    },
    data => {
        /* effect function */
    },
);

const disposer3 = when(
```

```
    () => {
        /* predicate function */
    },
    predicate => {
        /* effect function */
    },
);

// Dispose pre-maturely
disposer1();
disposer2();
disposer3();
```

Going back to the preceding diagram on the decision-tree, we can now define what it means to be *long-running*: the reaction does not dispose itself automatically after executing the first time. It continues to live until explicitly disposed using the *disposer-function*. autorun() and reaction() fall under the category of long-running reactions, whereas when() is one-time only. Note that when() also gives back a *disposer-function*, which can pre-maturely cancel the when() effect. However, the *one-time* behavior means that after the effect executes, when() will automatically dispose of itself, without requiring any clean up.

The second defining characteristic that is covered in the decision-tree is about *selecting the observables* to track. This is a guarding condition for the *effect-function* to execute. reaction() and when() have the ability to decide which observables to use for tracking, whereas, autorun() implicitly selects all observables in its *effect-function*. In the case of reaction() it's the *tracking-function*, and for when() it's the *predicate-function*. These functions are expected to produce a value, and when it changes, the *effect-function* is executed.

 The *selector-function* of reaction() and when() is where the observable tracking happens. The *effect-function* is only for causing side effects with no tracking. autorun() implicitly combines the *selector-function* and the *effect-function* into just one function.

Using the decision tree, you can classify the different *side effects* in your application. In Chapter 6, *Handling Real-World Use Cases*, we will look at various examples that will make this selection process more natural.

Configuring autorun() and reaction()

Both `autorun()` and `reaction()` offer an extra argument to customize the behavior a little more. Let's look at the most common properties that can be passed as options.

Options for autorun()

The second argument to `autorun()` is an object that carries the *options*:

```
autorun(() => { /* side effects */}, options)
```

It has the following properties:

- `name`: This is useful for debugging purposes, especially in the context of MobX DevTools, where the `name` is printed in the logs. The name is also used with the `spy()` utility function provided by MobX. Both of these will be covered in a later chapter.
- `delay`: This acts as a debouncer for frequently changing observables. The *effect-function* will wait for the `delay` period (specified in milliseconds) before re-executing. In the example shown next, we want to be careful not to fire a network request for every change to `profile.couponsUsed`. An easy guard is to use the `delay` option:

```
import { autorun } from 'mobx';

const profile = observable({
    name: 'Pavan Podila',
    id: 123,
    couponsUsed: 3,
});

function sendCouponTrackingAnalytics(id, couponsUsed) {
    /* Make network request */
}

autorun(
    () => {
        sendCouponTrackingAnalytics(profile.id,
profile.couponsUsed);
    },
    { delay: 1000 },
);
```

- onError: Errors thrown during the execution of the *effect-function* can be safely handled by providing the onError handler. The error is given as input to the onError handler, which can then be used to recover, and prevent the exceptional state for subsequent runs of the *effect-function*. Note that by providing this handler, MobX continues tracking even after an error occurs. This keeps the system running and allows other scheduled *side effects*, which are possibly unrelated, to run as expected.

In the following example, we have an onError handler that deals with cases where the number of coupons is greater than two. Providing this handler keeps the autorun() running without interfering with the rest of the MobX reactivity system. We are also removing the excess coupons to prevent this from happening again:

```
autorun(
    () => {
        if (profile.couponsUsed > 2) {
            throw new Error('No more than 2 Coupons allowed');
        }
    },
    {
        onError(ex) {
            console.error(ex);
            removeExcessCoupons(profile.id);
        },
    },
);

function removeExcessCoupons(id) {}
```

Options for reaction()

Similar to autorun(), we can pass an extra argument to reaction() that contains the *options*:

```
reaction(() => {/* tracking data */}, (data) => { /* side effects */},
                        options)
```

Some of the options, as shown below, are exactly like *autorun*, which keeps it consistent:

- name
- delay
- onError

However, there are additional options, specifically for `reaction()`:

- `fireImmediately`: This is a boolean value that indicates whether the *effect-function* should be triggered immediately after the first invocation of the *tracking-function*. Notice that this behavior gets us closer to `autorun()`, which also runs immediately. By default, it is set to `false`.
- `equals`: Notice that the *tracking-function* in a `reaction()` gives back `data` that is used to compare with the previously produced value. For primitive values, the default *equality comparison* (`comparer.default`), which is based on value, works well. However, you are free to supply a structural comparer (`comparer.structural`) to ensure a deeper comparison is performed. The equality check is important, because only when the values (produced by *tracking-function*) differ, will the *effect-function* be invoked.

When does MobX react?

The MobX reactivity system starts with the tracking or observation of the *observables*. This is an important aspect of building the reactivity graph, so tracking the correct observables is key. By following a simple set of rules, you can guarantee the outcome of the tracking process and ensure your reactions fire correctly.

We will use the term *tracking-function* to mean any one of the following:

- The function passed into `autorun()`. The observables used in that function are tracked by MobX.
- The *selector-function* (first argument) of a `reaction()` or `when()`. The observables used in it are tracked.
- The `render()` method of an *observer*-React-component. The observables used during the execution of the `render()` method are tracked.

The rules

With each of the following rules, we will look at an example of the rule in action:

- Always dereference observables during the execution of the tracking-function. Dereferencing is the key to establishing the MobX tracker.

```
const item = observable({
    name: 'Laptop',
    price: 999,
```

```
                    quantity: 1,
            });

            autorun(() => {
                showInfo(item);
            });

            item.price = 1050;
```

In the preceding snippet, the `autorun()` is not invoked again since there is no observable property being dereferenced. For MobX to react to changes, it needs an observable property being read inside the *tracking-function*. One possible fix is to read the `item.price` inside the `autorun()`, which will re-trigger anytime `item.price` is changed:

```
autorun(() => {
    showInfo(item.price);
});
```

- Tracking only happens in the synchronously executing code of the tracking-function:
    - The observables should be accessed directly in the tracking-function and not in an async function inside.
    - In the following code, MobX will never react to the change in `item.quantity`. Although we are dereferencing the observable inside `autorun()`, it is not being done synchronously. Hence, MobX will never re-execute `autorun()`:

```
autorun(() => {
    setTimeout(() => {
        if (item.quantity > 10) {
            item.price = 899;
        }
    }, 500);
});

item.quantity = 24;
```

To fix, we can pull the code out from the `setTimeout()` and place it directly inside `autorun()`. If the use of `setTimeout()` is to add some delayed execution, we can do that with the `delay` option of `autorun()`. The following code shows the fix:

```
autorun(
    () => {
        if (item.quantity > 10) {
            item.price = 899;
        }
```

```
    },
    { delay: 500 },
);
```

- Only observables that already exist will be tracked:
  - In the following example, we are dereferencing an observable (a computed property), which does not exist on the item at the time autorun() executes. Hence, MobX never tracks it. Later in the code, we are changing the item.quantity, resulting in a change in item.description, but autorun() still doesn't execute:

```
autorun(() => {
    console.log(`Item Description: ${item.description}`);
});

extendObservable(item, {
    get description() {
        return `Only ${item.quantity} left at
$${item.price}`;
    },
});

item.quantity = 10;
```

An easy fix is to ensure the observable actually exists before autorun() executes. By changing the order of statements, we can get the desired behavior, as seen in the following snippet. In practice, you should declare upfront all the properties you will need. This helps MobX to track properties correctly when required, helps type-checkers (for example, TypeScript) ensure the correct properties are being used, and also expresses the intent clearly to the readers of your code:

```
extendObservable(item, {
    get description() {
        return `Only ${item.quantity} left at $${item.price}`;
    },
});

autorun(() => {
    console.log(`Item Description: ${item.description}`);
});

item.quantity = 10;
```

In the snippet *before the fix*, if we had also read the `item.quantity` in `autorun()`, then this *tracking-function* would re-execute on changes to `item.quantity`. That happens as the observable property exists at the time the `autorun()` executes for the first time. The second time `autorun()` executes (due to change in `item.quantity`), `item.description` would also be available and MobX can start tracking that as well.

- One exception to the previous rule is for Observable Maps where a dynamic key is also tracked:

```
const twitterUrls = observable.map({
    John: 'twitter.com/johnny',
});

autorun(() => {
    console.log(twitterUrls.get('Sara'));
});

twitterUrls.set('Sara', 'twitter.com/horsejs');
```

In the preceding code snippet, `autorun()` will re-execute since `twitterUrls` is an `observable.map`, which tracks the addition of new keys. Thus, the key, `Sara`, is still tracked even though it is non-existent at the time `autorun()` executes.

In MobX 5, it can track *not-yet-existing* properties for all objects created using the `observable()` API.

Summary

The mental model for MobX apps is geared towards thinking about the *observable state*. This itself is divided into the *minimal core state* and a *derived state*. Derivations are how we handle the various projections of the core state onto the UI and places where we need to perform domain-specific operations. Before adding more core state, think about whether it can be rolled in as derived state. Only when that is not possible should you introduce new core state.

We saw how an *async action* is quite similar to a regular *action* without much ceremony. The only caveat is when you have configured MobX to `enforceActions`. In that case, you have to wrap *state mutations* in the async code inside `runInAction()`. When there are several async parts within the action, `flow()` is a better option. It takes a generator function (denoted by `function*(){ }`) that is interspersed with `yield` to the various *promise-based* calls.

`reaction()` and `autorun()` offer extra options to control their behavior. They share most of the options, such as *name, delay,* and *onError.* `reaction()` has two more options: to control how comparisons are made on the data produced by the *tracking-function* (`equals`), and if the *effect-function* should be fired immediately after the first run of the *tracking-function* (`fireImmediately`).

In `Chapter 6`, *Handling Real-World Use Cases*, we can start exploring approaches to tackling various common scenarios with MobX. If the chapters until now seemed like *science*, the next one is *applied-science*!

6
Handling Real-World Use Cases

Applying the principles of MobX can seem daunting when you first start using it. To help you with this process, we are gong to tackle two non-trivial examples of using the MobX triad of *observables-actions-reactions*. We will cover the modeling of the observable state, and then identify the actions and the reactions that track the observables. Once you go through these examples, you should be able to make the mental shift in tackling state management with MobX.

The examples we will cover in this chapter include the following:

- Form validation
- Page routing

Technical requirements

You will be required to have JavaScript programming language. Finally, to use the Git repository of this book, the user needs to install Git.

The code files of this chapter can be found on GitHub:

https://github.com/PacktPublishing/Mobx-Quick-Start-Guide/tree/master/src/Chapter06

Check out the following video to see the code in action:
http://bit.ly/2LDliA9

Form validation

Filling up forms and validating fields is the classic use-case of the web. So, it's fitting we start here and see how MobX can help us simplify it. For our example, we will consider a User Enrollment form that takes in some standard inputs like first name, last name, email, and password.

The various states of enrollment are captured in the following figure:

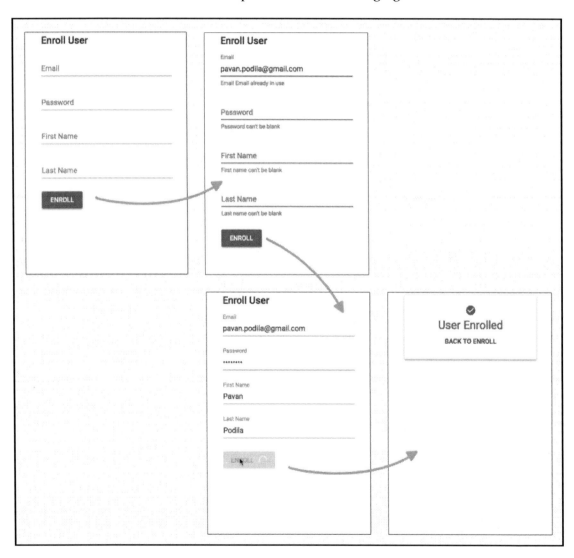

The interactions

Looking at the preceding screenshot, we can see some standard interactions going on, such as:

- Entering inputs for various fields
- Validation on those fields
- Clicking the **Enroll** button to perform a network operation

There are few other interactions here that do not meet the eye immediately:

- Network-based validation for the email to ensure that we are not registering with an existing email address
- Showing a progress indicator for the enroll operation

Many of these interactions will be modeled with actions and reactions in MobX. The state will, of course, be modeled with observables. Let's see how the *Observables-Actions-Reactions* triad comes to life in this example.

Modeling the observable state

The visual design for the example already hints at the core state that we need. This includes the firstName, lastName, email, and password fields. We can model these as *observable properties* of the UserEnrollmentData class.

Additionally, we also need to track the async validation that will happen with email. We do that with the boolean validating property. Any errors that are found during the validation are tracked with errors. Finally, the enrollmentStatus tracks the network operation around enrollment. It is a string-enum that can have one of four values: none, pending, completed, or failed:

```
class UserEnrollmentData {
    @observable email = '';
    @observable password = '';
    @observable firstName = '';
    @observable lastName = '';
    @observable validating = false;
    @observable.ref errors = null;
    @observable enrollmentStatus = 'none'; // none | pending | completed |
failed
}
```

You will notice that `errors` is marked with `@observable.ref`, as it only needs to track reference changes. This is because the validation output is an *opaque object*, which does not have anything observable besides a change in reference. Only when `errors` has a value do we know that there are validation errors.

Onto the actions

The actions here are quite straightforward. We need one to *set the field value* based on user changes. The other is do *enrollment* when the **Enroll** button is clicked. These two can be seen in the following code.

As a general practice, always start with a call to `configure({ enforceActions:` `'strict' })`. This ensures that your observables are only mutated inside an action, giving you all the benefits we discussed in Chapter 5, *Derivations, Actions, and Reactions*:

```
import { action, configure, flow } from 'mobx';

configure({ enforceActions: 'strict' });

class UserEnrollmentData {
    /* ... */

    @action
    setField(field, value) {
        this[field] = value;
    }

    getFields() {
        const { firstName, lastName, password, email } = this;
        return { firstName, lastName, password, email }
    }

    enroll = flow(function*() {
        this.enrollmentStatus = 'pending';
        try {
            // Validation
            const fields = this.getFields();
            yield this.validateFields(fields);
            if (this.errors) {
                throw new Error('Invalid fields');
            }

            // Enrollment
            yield enrollUser(fields);
```

```
                this.enrollmentStatus = 'completed';
        } catch (e) {
                this.enrollmentStatus = 'failed';
        }
    });

}
```

The use of `flow()` for the `enroll` action is deliberate. We are dealing with async operations internally, so the mutations that happen after the operation completes must be wrapped in `runInAction()` or an `action()`. Doing this manually can be cumbersome and also adds noise to the code.

With `flow()`, you get clean looking code by using a generator function with `yield` statements for the `promises`. In the preceding code, we have two `yield` points, one for `validateFields()` and the other for `enroll()`, both of which return `promises`. Notice that we have no wrapper code after these statements, making it easier to follow the logic.

One other action that is implicit here is `validateFields()`. Validation is actually a side effect that is triggered any time the fields change, but can also be invoked directly as an action. Here, again, we use `flow()` to handle the mutations after running through the async validations:

 We are using the `validate.js` (`https://validatejs.org`) NPM package to handle the field validations.

```
import Validate from 'validate.js';

class UserEnrollmentData {

    /* ... */

    validateFields = flow(function*(fields) {
        this.validating = true;
        this.errors = null;

        try {
            yield Validate.async(fields, rules);

            this.errors = null;
        } catch (err) {
            this.errors = err;
        } finally {
            this.validating = false;
```

```
        }
    });

    /* ... */
  }
```

Notice how the `flow()` can take in arguments (eg: `fields`) just like regular functions. Since the validation for email involves an async operation, we are tracking the entire validation as an async operation. We do this with the `validating` property. When the operation completes, we set it back to `false` in the `finally` block.

Completing the triad with reactions

When the fields are changed, we need to ensure that the values that have been entered are valid. Thus, validation is a side effect of entering values for the various fields. We know that MobX offers three ways in which you can handle this side effect, and they are `autorun()`, `reaction()`, and `when()`. Since validation is an effect that should be performed every time a field changes, `when()`, a one-time only effect, can be ruled out. That leaves us with `reaction()` and `autorun()`. Typically, a form will only validate when a field has actually changed. This means the effect needs to trigger only after a change.

That narrows down our choice to `reaction(<tracking-function>, <effect-function>)`, as that's the only type of reaction that ensures the `effect` function triggers after the `tracking` function returns a different value. `autorun()`, on the other hand, executes immediately, which is too soon to perform validation. With that, we can now introduce the *validation* side effect in the `UserEnrollmentData` class:

 Technically, this could also be achieved with an `autorun()`, but will require an additional boolean flag to ensure the validation is not performed the first time. Either solution would work well in this situation.

```
class UserEnrollmentData {

    disposeValidation = null;

    constructor() {
        this.setupValidation();
    }

    setupValidation() {
        this.disposeValidation = reaction(
```

```
        () => {
            const { firstName, lastName, password, email } = this;
            return { firstName, lastName, password, email };
        },
        () => {
            this.validateFields(this.getFields());
        },
    );
}

/* ... */

cleanup() {
    this.disposeValidation();
}
}
```

The tracking function in the preceding reaction() picks up the fields to monitor. When any of them change, the tracking function produces a new value, which then triggers the validation. We have already seen the validateFields() method, which is also an action that uses flow(). The reaction() is set up in the constructor of UserEnrollmentData, so the monitoring starts immediately.

 When this.validateFields() is called, it gives back a promise, which could be canceled prematurely using its cancel() method. If validateFields() gets called too frequently, a previous invocation of the method could still be in progress. In those cases, we could cancel() the previously returned promise to avoid unnecessary work.

We will leave it as a reader exercise to tackle this interesting use-case.

We also keep track of the disposer function returned by the reaction(), which we call inside cleanup(). This is required to clean up and avoid potential memory leaks when UserEnrollmentData is no longer needed. It is always good to have an exit point for reactions where its *disposer* gets called. In our case, we call cleanup() from the root React component, in its componentWillUnmount() hook. We will see that in the next section.

Now, validation is not the only side effect of our example. The more grandiose side effect is the UI in the form of React components.

React components

The UI as we know is a side effect in MobX and is identified by the use of `observer()` decorators on the React components. These observers can read observables in the `render()` method, which sets up the tracking. Any time those observables change, MobX will re-render the component. This automatic behavior with minimal ceremony is very powerful and allows us to create granular components that react to fine-grained observable state.

In our example, we do have some granular observer components, namely the input fields, the enroll button, and the app component. They are marked by orange boxes in the following component tree:

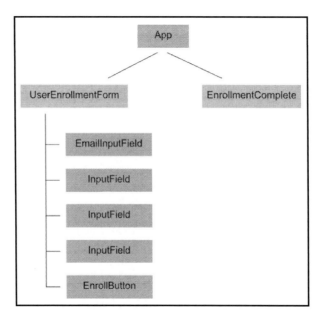

Each field input is separated out into an observer component: **InputField**. The email field has its own component, **EmailInputField**, since its visual feedback also involves showing a progress bar during validation and disabling it while it checks if the entered email is registered already. Similarly, the **EnrollButton** also has a spinner to show the progress during the enroll operation.

We are using **Material-UI** (`https://material-ui.com`) as the component library. This provides an excellent set of React components styled to the Material Design guidelines by Google.

The `InputField` observes just the field that it is rendering, identified by the `field` prop, which is dereferenced from the `store` prop (using `store[field]`). This serves as the value for the `InputField`:

```
const InputField = observer(({ store, field, label, type }) => {
    const errors = store.errors && store.errors[field];
    const hasError = !!errors;

    return (
        <TextField
            fullWidth
            type={type}
            value={store[field]}
            label={label}
            error={hasError}
            onChange={event => store.setField(field,
            event.target.value)}
            margin={'normal'}
            helperText={errors ? errors[0] : null}
        />
    );
});
```

User edits (`onChange` event) to this input are notified back to the store with the `store.setField()` action. The `InputField` is a *controlled component* in the React parlance.

The key idea of the `InputField` component is about passing the observable (`store`) instead of the value (`store[field]`). This ensures the dereferencing of the observable property happens inside the `render()` of the component. This is important for a granular observer optimized for rendering and tracking just what it needs. You can think of it as a *design pattern* when creating MobX observer components.

The UserEnrollmentForm component

We use several of these `InputFields` in the `UserEnrollmentForm` component. Note that the `UserEnrollmentForm` component *is not an observer*. Its purpose is to get hold of the store via the `inject()` decorator and pass it down to some of its child *observer components*. The `inject()` here uses the *function-based* argument, which is more type-safe than the *string-based* argument of `inject('store')`:

```
import React from 'react';
import { inject } from 'mobx-react';
import { Grid, TextField, Typography, } from '@material-ui/core';
```

```
@inject(stores => ({ store: stores.store }))
class UserEnrollmentForm extends React.Component {
    render() {
        const { store } = this.props;
        return (
            <form>
                <Grid container direction={'column'}>
                    <CenteredGridItem>
                        <Typography variant={'title'}>Enroll
                        User</Typography>
                    </CenteredGridItem>

                    <CenteredGridItem>
                        <EmailInputField store={store} />
                    </CenteredGridItem>

                    <CenteredGridItem>
                        <InputField
                            type={'password'}
                            field={'password'}
                            label={'Password'}
                            store={store}
                        />
                    </CenteredGridItem>

                    <CenteredGridItem>
                        <InputField
                            type={'text'}
                            field={'firstName'}
                            label={'First Name'}
                            store={store}
                        />
                    </CenteredGridItem>

                    <CenteredGridItem>
                        <InputField
                            type={'text'}
                            field={'lastName'}
                            label={'Last Name'}
                            store={store}
                        />
                    </CenteredGridItem>

                    <CenteredGridItem>
                        <EnrollButton store={store} />
                    </CenteredGridItem>
                </Grid>
            </form>
```

```
                );
        }
    }
```

The `store`, an instance of `UserEnrollmentData`, is passed down via the `Provider` component setup at the root of the component tree. This is created in the `constructor` for the root component:

```
import React from 'react';
import { UserEnrollmentData } from './store';
import { Provider } from 'mobx-react';
import { App } from './components';

export class FormValidationExample extends React.Component {
    constructor(props) {
        super(props);

        this.store = new UserEnrollmentData();
    }

    render() {
        return (
            <Provider store={this.store}>
                <App />
            </Provider>
        );
    }

    componentWillUnmount() {
        this.store.cleanup();
        this.store = null;
    }
}
```

With the `Provider`, any component can now `inject()` the `store` and get access to the observable state. Notice the use of the `componentWillUnmount()` hook to invoke `this.store.cleanup()`. This internally disposes the validation reaction, as described in the earlier section (*"Completing the triad with reactions"*).

Other observer components

There are a few more granular observers in our component tree. One of the simplest ones is the App component, which provides a simple branching logic. If we are still in the process of enrolling, the UserEnrollmentForm is shown. Upon enrollment, the App shows the EnrollmentComplete component. The observable tracked here is store.enrollmentStatus:

```
@inject('store')
@observer
export class App extends React.Component {
    render() {
        const { store } = this.props;
        return store.enrollmentStatus === 'completed' ? (
            <EnrollmentComplete />
        ) : (
            <UserEnrollmentForm />
        );
    }
}
```

The EmailInputField is fairly self-explanatory and reuses the InputField component. It also includes a progress bar to show the async validation operation:

```
const EmailInputField = observer(({ store }) => {
    const { validating } = store;

    return (
        <Fragment>
            <InputField
                type={'text'}
                store={store}
                field={'email'}
                label={'Email'}
            />
            {validating ? <LinearProgress variant={'query'} /> : null}
        </Fragment>
    );
});
```

And finally, the last observer component is the `EnrollButton`, which observes the `enrollmentStatus` and fires the `enroll()` action on the `store`. While the enrollment is in progress, it also shows the circular spinner:

```
const EnrollButton = observer(({ store }) => {
    const isEnrolling = store.enrollmentStatus === 'pending';
    const failed = store.enrollmentStatus === 'failed';

    return (
        <Fragment>
            <Button
                variant={'raised'}
                color={'primary'}
                style={{ marginTop: 20 }}
                disabled={isEnrolling}
                onClick={() => store.enroll()}
            >
                Enroll
                {isEnrolling ? (
                    <CircularProgress
                        style={{
                            color: 'white',
                            marginLeft: 10,
                        }}
                        size={20}
                        variant={'indeterminate'}
                    />
                ) : null}
            </Button>
            {failed ? (
                <Typography color={'secondary'} variant={'subheading'}>
                    Failed to enroll
                </Typography>
            ) : null}{' '}
        </Fragment>
    );
});
```

The collection of these granular observers improves the efficiency of the UI by speeding up React's reconciliation process. As the changes are localized to a specific component, React only has to reconcile the virtual-DOM changes for that specific observer component. MobX encourages the use of such granular observers and sprinkling them throughout your component tree.

 If you are looking for a library built specifically for form validation with MobX, look at *mobx-react-form* (`https://github.com/foxhound87/mobx-react-form`).

Page routing

Single page apps (SPA) have become commonplace in many of the web apps we see today. These apps are characterised by the use of logical, client-side routes within a single page. You can navigate to various parts (*routes*) of the application by modifying the URL without a full page load. This is handled by libraries such as `react-router-dom`, which works with the browser history to enable *URL* driven route changes.

Route change or navigation can be treated as a *side effect* in the MobX world. There is some state change happening to the observables, which results in navigation happening in the SPA. In this example, we will build this observable state, which tracks the current page shown in the browser. Using a combination of `react-router-dom` and the `history` package, we will show how routing becomes a side effect of the change in observable state.

The Cart checkout workflow

Let's look at a use-case where we can see the route change (navigation) as a MobX-driven side effect. We will use the typical Cart checkout workflow as our example. As seen in the following screenshot, we start at the *home route*, which is the entry point of the workflow. From there, we go through the remaining steps: *viewing the cart, selecting a payment option, seeing the confirmation*, and then *tracking the order*:

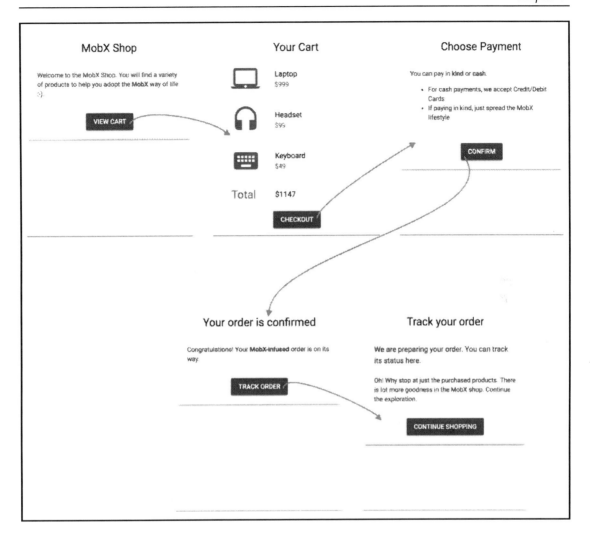

We have deliberately kept the various steps visually simple. This allows us to focus more on the navigation aspect rather than the details of what happens within each step. However, there are certain elements that are *common across all of these steps* of the workflow.

As seen in the following screenshot, each step has a load operation that fetches details for that step. Once loaded, you can click on the button to go to the next step. Before the navigation happens, there is an async operation that is performed. After it completes, we navigate to the next step in the workflow. Since every step follows this template, we will model it as such in the next section:

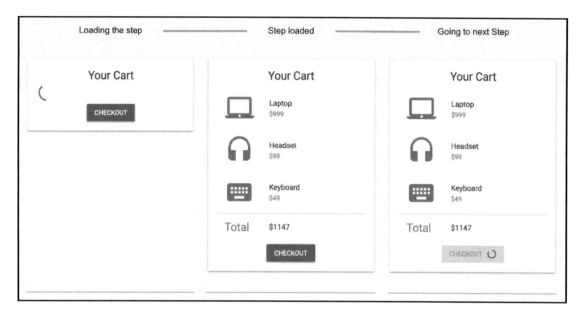

Modeling the observable state

The essence of this SPA is the checkout workflow that takes you step by step, where each step is a route. Since a route is driven by a URL, we need a way to monitor the URL and also have the ability to change it as we move between steps. The navigation between steps is a side effect of some change in the observable state. We will model this workflow with a CheckoutWorkflow class that contains the core observable state:

```
const routes = {
    shopping: '/',
    cart: '/cart',
    payment: '/payment',
    confirm: '/confirm',
    track: '/track',
};

export class CheckoutWorkflow {
    static steps = [
```

```
            { name: 'shopping', stepClass: ShoppingStep },
            { name: 'cart', stepClass: ShowCartStep },
            { name: 'payment', stepClass: PaymentStep },
            { name: 'confirm', stepClass: ConfirmStep },
            { name: 'track', stepClass: TrackStep },
        ];

        tracker = new HistoryTracker();
        nextStepPromise = null;

        @observable currentStep = null;
        @observable.ref step = null;

}
```

As can be seen in the preceding code, we are representing each of the steps with a `name` and a `stepClass`. The `name` is also how we identify the corresponding route for that step, stored in the singleton `routes` object. The ordered list of `steps` is stored as a static property of the `CheckoutWorkflow` class. We could have also loaded these steps from a separate JavaScript file (module), but for simplicity, we have kept it here.

The core observable state is quite simple here: a `currentStep` property that stores the string name of the current step and a `step` property, an instance of the `stepClass`, stored as an `observable.ref` property. As we navigate between steps, these two properties change to reflect the current step. We will see how these properties are used in handling the route change.

A route for a step, a step for a route

You may be wondering why we need two separate properties to track the current step. Yes, it may seem superfluous, but there is a reason for that. Since our workflow is going to be a set of url-routes, the change in route can also happen by using the back button of the browser or by directly typing a URL. One way to co-relate a route with a step is by using its *name*, which is exactly what we do with the `currentStep` property. Notice how the `name` of the step exactly matches the keys of the `routes` object.

When a route changes externally, we rely on the browser history to notify us of the URL change. The `tracker` property, which is an instance of `HistoryTracker` (a custom class we will create), contains the logic to listen to *browser history* and track the current URL in the browser. It exposes an observable property that is tracked by the `CheckoutWorkflow`. We will look at its implementation a little later in this chapter:

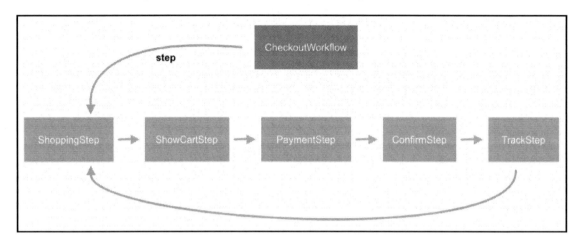

Each step in the `CheckoutWorkflow` is a subtype of a `WorkflowStep` class. The `WorkflowStep` captures the details of a step and its async operations. The workflow simply orchestrates the flow of steps and transitions between them upon completion of the async operation in each step:

```
class ShowCartStep extends WorkflowStep { /* ... */}

// A mock step to simplify the representation of other steps
class MockWorkflowStep extends WorkflowStep { /* ... */ }

class PaymentStep extends MockWorkflowStep { /* ... */ }
class ConfirmStep extends MockWorkflowStep { /* ... */ }
class TrackStep extends MockWorkflowStep { /* ... */ }
```

For most of the steps, we are extending the `MockWorkflowStep` that stamps out a template `WorkflowStep` with some baked in defaults. This keeps the steps really simple, so we can focus on the routing between steps. Notice in the following snippet, where we are simply simulating a network delay for the `load` and `main` operations. The `delay()` function is just a simple helper that returns a `Promise` that resolves after the given millisecond interval.

We will see how the `getLoadOperation()` and `getMainOperation()` methods are used in the next section:

```
class MockWorkflowStep extends WorkflowStep {
    getLoadOperation() {
        return delay(1000);
    }

    getMainOpcration() {
        return delay(1000);
    }
}

function delay(ms) {
    return new Promise(resolve => setTimeout(resolve, ms));
}
```

The WorkflowStep

The `WorkflowStep` acts as a template for all the steps in the workflow. It contains some observable state to keep track of the two async operations it performs: *loading details* and *doing the main work*:

```
class WorkflowStep {
    workflow = null; // the parent workflow
    @observable loadState = 'none'; // pending | completed | failed
    @observable operationState = 'none'; // pending | completed |
     failed

    async getLoadOperation() {}
    async getMainOperation() {}

    @action.bound
    async load() {
        doAsync(
            () => this.getLoadOperation(),
            state => (this.loadState = state),
        );
    }

    @action.bound
    async perform() {
        doAsync(
            () => this.getMainOperation(),
            state => (this.operationState = state),
        );
```

```
        }
    }
```

`load()` and `perform()` are the two async operations that a `WorkflowStep` does. Their status is tracked with the `loadState` and `operationState` observables, respectively. Each of these operations calls a delegate method that is overridden by the subclass to provide the actual promise. `load()` calls `getLoadOperation()` and `perform()` calls `getMainOperation()`, each of which produces a promise.

`doAsync()` is a helper function that takes in a *promise function* and notifies the state using the passed-in callback (`setState`). Notice the use of `runInAction()` here to ensure all mutations happen inside an action.

`load()` and `perform()` use the `doAsync()` function to update the `loadState` and `operationState` observables appropriately:

 There is a different way of writing the `doAsync()` function. **Hint**: We have seen it in an earlier chapter. We'll leave that as an exercise for the reader.

```
async function doAsync(getPromise, setState) {
    setState('pending');
    try {
        await getPromise();
        runInAction(() => {
            setState('completed');
        });
    } catch (e) {
        runInAction(() => {
            setState('failed');
        });
    }
}
```

We can now see that the observable state is carried by the `CheckoutWorkflow` and the `WorkflowStep` instances. One thing that may not be clear is how the orchestration is performed by the `CheckoutWorkflow`. For that, we have to look at the actions and reactions.

Actions and reactions of the workflow

We have already seen that the `WorkflowStep` has two *action* methods, `load()` and `perform()`, that handle the async operations of the step:

```
class WorkflowStep {
    workflow = null;
    @observable loadState = 'none'; // pending | completed | failed
    @observable operationState = 'none'; // pending | completed |
     failed

    async getLoadOperation() {}
    async getMainOperation() {}

    @action.bound
    async load() {
        doAsync(
            () => this.getLoadOperation(),
            state => (this.loadState = state),
        );
    }

    @action.bound
    async perform() {
        doAsync(
            () => this.getMainOperation(),
            state => (this.operationState = state),
        );
    }
}
```

The `load()` action is invoked by `CheckoutWorkflow` as it loads each step of the workflow. `perform()` is a user invoked action that happens when the user clicks the button exposed on the React component for the step. Once `perform()` completes, the `operationState` will change to `completed`. The `CheckoutWorkflow` tracks this and automatically loads the next step in sequence. In other words, the workflow progresses as a reaction (or side effect) to the change in `operationState` of the current step. Let's see all of this in the following set of code snippets:

```
export class CheckoutWorkflow {
    /* ... */

    tracker = new HistoryTracker();
    nextStepPromise = null;

    @observable currentStep = null;
```

```
@observable.ref step = null;

constructor() {
    this.tracker.startListening(routes);

    this.currentStep = this.tracker.page;

    autorun(() => {
        const currentStep = this.currentStep;

        const stepIndex = CheckoutWorkflow.steps.findIndex(
            x => x.name === currentStep,
        );

        if (stepIndex !== -1) {
            this.loadStep(stepIndex);

            this.tracker.page = CheckoutWorkflow.steps[stepIndex].name;
        }
    });

    reaction(
        () => this.tracker.page,
        page => {
            this.currentStep = page;
        },
    );
}

@action
async loadStep(stepIndex) {
    /* ... */
}
}
```

The constructor of `CheckoutWorkflow` sets up the core side effects. The first thing we need to know is the current page served by the browser using `this.tracker.page`. Remember that we are co-relating the `currentStep` of the workflow with the current URL-based route using a shared name.

The first side effect is executed using autorun(), which as we know, runs immediately and then any time the tracked observables change. Inside the autorun(), we are loading the currentStep by first making sure it is a valid step. Since we are observing the currentStep inside the autorun(), we have to ensure that we are keeping this.tracker.page in sync. We do this after successfully loading the current step. Now, any time the currentStep changes, tracker.page is automatically brought in sync, which means that the URL and route update to reflect the current step. We will see a little later how the tracker, an instance of HistoryTracker, actually handles this internally.

The next side effect is the reaction() to the change in tracker.page. This is a counterpart to the previous side effect. Any time the tracker.page changes, we have to change the currentStep as well. After all, these two observables have to work in tandem. Because we are already tracking the currentStep with a separate side effect (the autorun()), the current step is loaded with the instance of the WorkflowStep.

One thing striking over here is that, when currentStep changes, tracker.page is updated. Also, when tracker.page changes, currentStep is updated. So, it may appear that there is an infinite loop here:

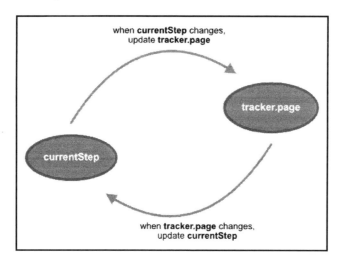

However, MobX will see that once the change is propagated in one direction, there is no update happening from the other side, as both are in sync. This means the two interdependent values quickly reach stability and there is no infinite loop.

Loading a step

The `WorkflowStep` is where a step comes to life and the only one that can create an instance is the `CheckoutWorkflow`. After all, it is the owner of the entire workflow. It does this in the `loadStep()` action method:

```
export class CheckoutWorkflow {
    /* ... */

    @action
    async loadStep(stepIndex) {
        if (this.nextStepPromise) {
            this.nextStepPromise.cancel();
        }

        const StepClass = CheckoutWorkflow.steps[stepIndex].stepClass;
        this.step = new StepClass();
        this.step.workflow = this;
        this.step.load();
        this.nextStepPromise = when(
            () => this.step.operationState === 'completed',
        );

        await this.nextStepPromise;

        const nextStepIndex = stepIndex + 1;
        if (nextStepIndex >= CheckoutWorkflow.steps.length) {
            return;
        }

        this.currentStep = CheckoutWorkflow.steps[nextStepIndex].name;
    }
}
```

The interesting parts of the preceding code are outlined as follows:

- We get the `stepClass` of the current step index by retrieving it from the list of steps. We create an instance of this `stepClass`, which is assigned to the observable `step` property.
- We then trigger the `load()` of the `WorkflowStep`.
- Possibly the most interesting part is awaiting the change in `operationState` of the `step`. We know from earlier that the `operationState` tracks the status of the main async operation of the step. Once it becomes `completed`, we know it's time to move to the next step.

- Notice the use of the `when()` with a promise. This gives us a nice way to demarcate code that needs to execute after the `when()` resolves. Also notice that we are keeping track of the promise in the `nextStepPromise` property. This is needed to ensure that we also `cancel` out the promise in case we move to a different step before the current step completes. It is worth pondering when this situation could arise. **Hint**: The flow of steps is not always linear. A step could be changed via a *route change* as well, such as by clicking the back button of the browser!

The HistoryTracker

The last piece of the *observable state puzzle* is the `HistoryTracker`, a class dedicated to monitoring the browser's URL and history. It relies on the `history` NPM package (`https://github.com/ReactTraining/history`) to do most of the work. The *history* package also powers the `react-router-dom` library, which we will be using for our React components.

The core responsibility of `HistoryTracker` is to expose an observable called `page` that tracks the current URL (route) in the browser. It also does the reverse where it keeps the URL in sync with the current `page`:

```
import createHashHistory from 'history/createHashHistory';
import { observable, action, reaction } from 'mobx';

export class HistoryTracker {
    unsubscribe = null;
    history = createHashHistory();

    @observable page = null;

    constructor() {
        reaction(
            () => this.page,
            page => {
                const route = this.routes[page];
                if (route) {
                    this.history.push(route);
                }
            },
        );
    }

    /* ... */
}
```

With the `reaction()` set up in the constructor, a route change (URL change) is effectively a side effect of a change in the `page` observable. This is achieved by pushing a route (URL) onto the browser history.

The other important aspect of `HistoryTracker`, as the name suggests, is tracking the browser history. This is done with the `startListening()` method, which can be invoked by the consumers of this class. The `CheckoutWorkflow` calls this in its constructor to set up the tracker. Note that `startListening()` is given a map of routes, with the `key` pointing to a URL path:

```
export class HistoryTracker {
    unsubscribe = null;
    history = createHashHistory();

    @observable page = null;

    startListening(routes) {
        this.routes = routes;
        this.unsubscribe = this.history.listen(location => {
            this.identifyRoute(location);
        });

        this.identifyRoute(this.history.location);
    }

    stopListening() {
        this.unsubscribe && this.unsubscribe();
    }

    @action
    setPage(key) {
        if (!this.routes[key]) {
            throw new Error(`Invalid Page: ${key}`);
        }

        this.page = key;
    }

    @action
    identifyRoute(location) {
        const { pathname } = location;
        const routes = this.routes;

        this.page = Object.keys(routes).find(key => {
            const path = routes[key];
            return path.startsWith(pathname);
        });
```

```
        }
    }
```

When the URL changes in the browser, the `page` observable is updated accordingly. This happens in the `identifyRoute()` method, which is called from the callback to `history.listen()`. We have decorated it with action since it *mutates* the `page` observable. Internally, MobX notifies all of the observers of `page`—for example, `CheckoutWorkflow`, which uses the `page` observable to update its `currentStep`. This keeps the whole routing in sync and ensures that the changes are bi-directional.

The following diagram shows the bi-directional syncing of the `currentStep`, `page`, and the *url-route*. Note that the interactions with the `history` package are shown in *grey* arrows, while the dependencies between observables are shown in orange arrows. This difference in color is intentional and suggests that *url-based-routing* is effectively a side effect of change in the observable state:

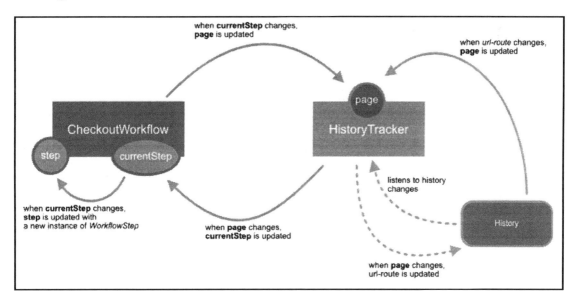

The React components

In this example, modeling of the observable state is more interesting than the React UI components. On the React side, we have the top level component that sets up the `Provider` with the instance of `CheckoutWorkflow` as the `store`. The `Provider` comes from the `mobx-react` package and helps in injecting the `store` to any React component decorated with `inject()`:

```
import React from 'react';
import ReactDOM from 'react-dom';
import { Provider } from 'mobx-react';
import { CheckoutWorkflow } from './CheckoutWorkflow';

const workflow = new CheckoutWorkflow();

export function PageRoutingExample() {
    return (
        <Provider store={workflow}>
            <App />
        </Provider>
    );
}
```

The `App` component simply sets up all the Routes using the `react-router-dom` package. The paths used in the `<Route />` components match the URLs we saw earlier on the `routes` object. Notice that the `history` from the `HistoryTracker` is used for the `Router`. This allows sharing of the browser history between *react-router* and *mobx*:

```
import React from 'react';
import ReactDOM from 'react-dom';
import { Route, Router, Switch } from 'react-router-dom';
import { CheckoutWorkflow } from './CheckoutWorkflow';
import { Paper } from '@material-ui/core/es/index';
import { ShowCart } from './show-cart';
import {
    ConfirmDescription,
    PaymentDescription,
    ShoppingDescription,
    TemplateStepComponent,
    TrackOrderDescription,
} from './shared';

const workflow = new CheckoutWorkflow();

class App extends React.Component {
    render() {
```

```
return (
    <Paper elevation={2} style={{ padding: 20 }}>
        <Router history={workflow.tracker.history}>
            <Switch>
                <Route
                    exact
                    path={'/'}
                    component={() => (
                        <TemplateStepComponent
                            title={'MobX Shop'}
                            renderDescription=
                            {ShoppingDescription}
                            operationTitle={'View Cart'}
                        />
                    )}
                />
                <Route exact path={'/cart'} component=
                    {ShowCart} />
                <Route
                    exact
                    path={'/payment'}
                    component={() => (
                        <TemplateStepComponent
                            title={'Choose Payment'}
                            renderDescription=
                            {PaymentDescription}
                            operationTitle={'Confirm'}
                        />
                    )}
                />
                <Route
                    exact
                    path={'/confirm'}
                    component={() => (
                        <TemplateStepComponent
                            title={'Your order is confirmed'}
                            operationTitle={'Track Order'}
                            renderDescription=
                             {ConfirmDescription}
                        />
                    )}
                />
                <Route
                    exact
                    path={'/track'}
                    component={() => (
                        <TemplateStepComponent
                            title={'Track your order'}
```

```
                                        operationTitle={'Continue
                                          Shopping'}
                                        renderDescription=
                                         {TrackOrderDescription}
                                     />
                                  )}
                               />
                             </Switch>
                          </Router>
                       </Paper>
                    );
                 }
              }
```

As mentioned earlier, we have deliberately kept the individual steps of the workflow very simple. They all follow a fixed template, as described by the `WorkflowStep`. Its React counterpart is `TemplateStepComponent`, which renders the step and exposes the button for navigating to the next step.

The TemplateStepComponent

`TemplateStepComponent` gives the visual representation to the `WorkflowStep`. It renders the feedback when the step is loading and also when the main operation is being performed. Additionally, it shows the details of the step once it is loaded. These details are shown via the `renderDetails` prop, which accepts a React component:

```
@inject('store')
export class TemplateStepComponent extends React.Component {
    static defaultProps = {
        title: 'Step Title',
        operationTitle: 'Operation',
        renderDetails: step => 'Some Description', // A render-prop to
render details of a step
    };

    render() {
        const { title, operationTitle, renderDetails } = this.props;

        return (
            <Fragment>
                <Typography
                    variant={'headline'}
                    style={{ textAlign: 'center' }}
                >
                    {title}
                </Typography>
```

```
    <Observer>
        {() => {
            const { step } = this.props.store;

            return (
                <OperationStatus
                    state={step.loadState}
                    render={() => (
                        <div style={{ padding: '2rem 0' }}>
                            {renderDetails(step)}
                        </div>
                    )}
                />
            );
        }}
    </Observer>

    <Grid justify={'center'} container>
        <Observer>
            {() => {
                const { step } = this.props.store;

                return (
                    <Button
                        variant={'raised'}
                        color={'primary'}
                        disabled={step.operationState ===
                            'pending'}
                        onClick={step.perform}>
                        {operationTitle}
                        {step.operationState === 'pending'
                            ? (
                            <CircularProgress
                                variant={'indeterminate'}
                                size={20}
                                style={{
                                    color: 'black',
                                    marginLeft: 10,
                                }}
                            />
                        ) : null}
                    </Button>
                );
            }}
        </Observer>
    </Grid>
</Fragment>
);
```

```
        }
    }
```

The `Observer` component is something we have not seen before. This is a special component provided by the `mobx-react` package that simplifies the creation of granular observers. A typical MobX observer component will require you to create a separate component, decorate it with `observer()` and/or `inject()` it, and ensure that the proper observables are passed as props into that component. You can bypass all that ceremony by simply wrapping a section of the *virtual-dom* with `<Observer />`.

It accepts a function as its only child, wherein you can read observables from the surrounding scope. MobX will automatically track the observables being used in the *function-as-child component*. A closer look at the `Observer` reveals these details:

```
<Observer>
    {() => {
        const { step } = this.props.store;

        return (
            <OperationStatus
                state={step.loadState}
                render={() => (
                    <div style={{ padding: '2rem 0' }}>
                        {renderDetails(step)}
                    </div>
                )}
            />
        );
    }}
</Observer>
```

In the preceding snippet, we are passing a function as the child to `<Observer />`. Within that function, we use the `step.loadState` observable. MobX automatically renders the *function-as-child* component when the `step.loadState` changes. Notice that we are not passing any props into the `Observer` or to the child component. It reads it directly from the props of the outer component. This is the advantage of using `Observer`. You can create anonymous observers without much effort.

A subtle point to note is that `TemplateStepComponent` is not an observer itself. It simply gets hold of the `store` with `inject()`, which is then used inside the `<Observer />` regions.

The ShowCart component

`ShowCart` is the component that shows the list of items in the cart. Here, we are reusing the `TemplateStepComponent` and plugin details of the cart with the `renderDetails` prop. This can be seen in the following code. We are not showing the `CartItem` and `TotalItem` components for simplicity. They are pure presentation components that render a single cart item:

```
import React from 'react';
import {
    List,
    ListItem,
    ListItemIcon,
    ListItemText,
    Typography,
} from '@material-ui/core';
import { Divider } from '@material-ui/core/es/index';
import { TemplateStepComponent } from './shared';

export class ShowCart extends React.Component {
    render() {
        return (
            <TemplateStepComponent
                title={'Your Cart'}
                operationTitle={'Checkout'}
                renderDetails={step => {
                    const { items, itemTotal } = step;

                    return (
                        <List>
                            {items.map(item => (
                                <CartItem key={item.title} item={item}
                                />
                            ))}

                            <Divider />

                            <TotalItem total={itemTotal} />
                        </List>
                    );
                }}
            />
        );
    }
}

function CartItem({ item }) {
```

```
    return (
        /* ... */
    );
}

function TotalItem({ total }) {
    return (
        /* ... */
    );
}
```

A state-based router

You can now see how the routing between all the `WorkflowStep` instances is achieved purely via a state-based approach. All of the navigation logic lies inside the MobX store, which in this case is `CheckoutWorkflow`. By connecting the observables (`tracker.page`, `currentStep`, and `step`) via a set of reactions, we have created *side effects* that update the browser history as well as create instances of `WorkflowStep`, which are used by the `TemplateStepComponent`.

Because we are sharing the browser history (via `HistoryTracker`) between `react-router-dom` and MobX, we can keep the observables in sync with the URL changes.

This state-based approach to routing helps in keeping a crisp mental model of the workflow. All of the logic of your feature stays inside the MobX Store, improving the readability. Writing *unit tests* for such a state-based solution is also straightforward. In fact, it is not surprising to have most of the unit tests in a MobX app to be centered around *stores* and *reactions*. Many of the React components become pure observers of the observables and can be treated as plain *presentation components*.

With MobX, you have the flexibility to focus squarely on the domain logic and ensure that there is appropriate *observable state* that can be rendered on the UI. By encapsulating all of the domain logic and state inside the stores, and all presentation in the React components, there is clear separation of concerns. This greatly improves the **developer experience** (**DX**) and helps you scale better over time. That is the true promise of MobX.

 For a more feature-rich, state-based routing solution with MobX, look at `mobx-state-router` (https://github.com/nareshbhatia/mobx-state-router).

Summary

In this chapter, we applied a variety of techniques and concepts that we have learned over the last few chapters. Each of the two examples, *form validation* and *page routing*, presented a unique set of approaches for modeling the observable state. We also saw how to create granular observer components to enable efficient rendering of the React components.

A practical application of MobX always starts with modeling the *observable state*. After all, that is the data that drives the UI. The next step is to identify the *actions* that mutate the observables. Finally, you need to call out the *side-effects* and see which observables these effects depend on. This is the side effect model that's applied to real-world scenarios, manifesting in the form of the MobX triad: *Observables-Actions-Reactions*.

With all of the knowledge we have accumulated so far, we are now ready to go deeper into MobX, starting with Chapter 7, *Special API for Special Cases*.

Special API for Special Cases

7

The MobX API surface is very lean and exposes the right abstractions for dealing with your state management logic. In most situations, the APIs we have seen thus far will suffice. However, there will always be those gnarly edge cases that demand a slight deviation from the well-trodden path. It is for these by-lanes for which MobX gives you some special APIs. We will look at some of these in this chapter.

The topics we will cover in this chapter include the following:

- Direct manipulation with the object API
- Using `inject()` and `observe()` to hook into the internal MobX eventing system
- Special utility functions and tools that will help in debugging
- Quick mention of some miscellaneous APIs

Technical requirements

You will be required to have JavaScript programming language. Finally, to use the Git repository of this book, the user needs to install Git.

The code files of this chapter can be found on GitHub:
`https://github.com/PacktPublishing/Mobx-Quick-Start-Guide/tree/master/src/Chapter07`

Check out the following video to see the code in action:
`http://bit.ly/2A1Or6V`

Direct manipulation with the object API

When deciding on the data structures for your observable state, your natural choice should be to reach out for observable.object(), observable.array(), observable.map(), observable.box(), or to use the convenient observable() API. Manipulating these data structures is as simple as mutating the properties directly or adding and removing elements as needed.

MobX gives you yet another way to surgically make changes to your data structures. It exposes a granular object API that can mutate these data structures at runtime. In fact, it gives you some capabilities that are not even possible with the original data structures. For example, adding new properties to observable objects and also keeping it reactive.

Granular reads and writes

The object API is focused on giving you granular control over the observable properties of top-level data structures: objects, arrays, and maps. In doing so, they continue to play well with the MobX reactive system and ensure the granular changes you make are picked up by the *reactions*. The following APIs apply to observable objects/arrays/maps:

- get(thing, key): Retrieves the value under the key. This key can even be non-existent. When used in a reaction, it will trigger a re-execution when that key becomes available.
- set(thing, key, value) or set(thing, { key: value }): sets a value for the key. The second form is better for setting multiple *key-value* pairs at once. Conceptually, it is very similar to Object.assign(), but with the addition of being reactive.
- has(thing, key): Gives back a boolean indicating if the key is present.
- remove(thing, key): Removes the given key and its value.
- values(thing): Gives an array of values.
- keys(thing): Gives an array containing all the keys. Note that this only applies to observable objects and maps.
- entries(thing): Gives back an array of key-value pairs, where each pair is an array of two elements ([key, value]).

The following snippet exercises all of these APIs:

```
import {
    autorun,
    observable,
    set,
    get,
    has,
    toJS,
    runInAction,
    remove,
    values,
    entries,
    keys,
} from 'mobx';

class Todo {
    @observable description = '';
    @observable done = false;

    constructor(description) {
        this.description = description;
    }
}

const firstTodo = new Todo('Write Chapter');
const todos = observable.array([firstTodo]);
const todosMap = observable.map({
    'Write Chapter': firstTodo,
});

// Reactions to track changes
autorun(() => {
    console.log(`metadata present: ${has(firstTodo, 'metadata')}`);
    console.log(get(firstTodo, 'metadata'), get(firstTodo, 'user'));
    console.log(keys(firstTodo));
});
autorun(() => {
    // Arrays
    const secondTodo = get(todos, 1);
    console.log('Second Todo:', toJS(secondTodo));
    console.log(values(todos), entries(todos));
});

// Granular changes
runInAction(() => {
    set(firstTodo, 'metadata', 'new Metadata');
    set(firstTodo, { metadata: 'meta update', user: 'Pavan Podila' });
```

```
        set(todos, 1, new Todo('Get it reviewed'));
});

runInAction(() => {
    remove(firstTodo, 'metadata');
    remove(todos, 1);
});
```

By using these APIs, you can target specific properties of the observables and update them as necessary. Reading and writing to keys that *don't exist* is considered valid with the object API. Notice how we read the metadata property of firstTodo in autorun(), which does not exist at the time of the call. However, MobX still tracks this key due to the use of the get() API. When we set() the metadata later in an action, autorun() is re-triggered to print it out on the console.

This can be seen in the following console output. Notice how the metadata check goes from false to true and back to false when removed:

```
metadata present: false
undefined undefined
(2) ["description", "done"]
Second Todo: undefined
[Todo] [Array(2)]

metadata present: true
meta update Pavan Podila
(4) ["description", "done", "metadata", "user"]
Second Todo: {description: "Get it reviewed", done: false}
(2) [Todo, Todo] (2) [Array(2), Array(2)]

metadata present: false
undefined "Pavan Podila"
(3) ["description", "done", "user"]
Second Todo: undefined
[Todo] [Array(2)]
```

From MobX to JavaScript

All of the observable types are special classes created by MobX that not only store data but also a bunch of housekeeping to track changes. We will explore this housekeeping in a later chapter, but for our discussion now, it suffices to say that these MobX types are not always compatible with other third-party APIs, especially when using MobX 4.

When interfacing with external libraries, you may need to send the raw JavaScript values instead of the MobX-typed values. This is where you need the toJS() function. It will convert the MobX observables to raw JavaScript values:

$$toJS(source, options?)$$

source: Any observable box, object, array, map, or primitives.

options: An optional argument to control behavior, such as:

- exportMapsAsObject (*boolean*): Whether to serialize the observable maps as objects (when true) or as JavaScript Maps (when false). Default is true.
- detectCycles (*boolean*): This is set to true by default. It detects cyclic references during serialization and reuses the already serialized object. This is a good default in most cases, but for performance reasons this can be set to false when you are sure of no cyclic references.

An important point to note with toJS() is that it does not serialize *computed properties*. This makes sense since it's purely derived information that can always be recomputed. The purpose of toJS() is to serialize the core observable state only. Similarly, any non-enumerable properties of the observable will not be serialized nor will they recurse into any non-observable data structures.

In the following example, you can see how the toJS() API is applied to observables:

```
const number = observable.box(10);
const cart = observable({
    items: [{ title: 'milk', quantity: 2 }, { title: 'eggs', quantity: 3
}],
});

console.log(toJS(number));

console.log('MobX type:', cart);
console.log('JS type:', toJS(cart));
```

The console output shows you the cart observable before and after applying the toJS() API:

```
10
MobX type: Proxy {Symbol(mobx administration):
ObservableObjectAdministration$$1}
JS type: {items: Array(2)}
```

Watching the events flow by

The APIs we have seen in the previous chapters allow you to create observables and react to the changes via *reactions*. MobX also gives you a way to tap into the events that flow internally to make the reactive system work. By attaching listeners to these events, you can fine-tune the use of some expensive resources or control which updates are allowed to be applied to the observables.

Hooking into the observability

Normally, *reactions* are the place where we read *observables* and apply some side effects. This tells MobX to start tracking the observable and re-trigger the reaction on changes. However, if we look at this from the *perspective* of the observable, how does it know when it is being used by a reaction? How can it do a one-time setup when it is read in a reaction and also clean up when it's no longer being used?

What we need here is the ability to know when an observable becomes *observed* and when it becomes *unobserved*: the two points in time where it becomes active and inactive in the MobX reactive system. For that, we have the following aptly named APIs:

- `disposer = onBecomeObserved(observable, property?: string, listener: () => void)`
- `disposer = onBecomeUnobserved(observable, property?: string, listener: () => void)`

`observable`: Can be a boxed observable, an observable object/array/map.

`property`: An optional property of the observable. Specifying a property is fundamentally different than referencing the property directly. For example, `onBecomeObserved(cart, 'totalPrice', () => {})` is different compared to `onBecomeObserved(cart.totalPrice, () => {})`. In the first case, MobX will be able to track the observable property but in the second case it won't, since it is only receiving the value rather than the property. In fact, MobX will throw an `Error`, indicating that there is nothing to track in the case of `cart.totalPrice`:

```
Error: [mobx] Cannot obtain atom from 0
```

The preceding error may not make much sense now, especially the term atom. We will look atoms in more detail in `Chapter 9`, *Mobx Internals*.

`disposer`: The return value of these handlers. This is a function that can be used to dispose these handlers and clean up the event wiring.

The following snippet shows these APIs in action:

```
import {
    onBecomeObserved,
    onBecomeUnobserved,
    observable,
    autorun,
} from 'mobx';

const obj = observable.box(10);
const cart = observable({
    items: [],
    totalPrice: 0,
});

onBecomeObserved(obj, () => {
    console.log('Started observing obj');
});

onBecomeUnobserved(obj, () => {
    console.log('Stopped observing obj');
});

onBecomeObserved(cart, 'totalPrice', () => {
    console.log('Started observing cart.totalPrice');
});
onBecomeUnobserved(cart, 'totalPrice', () => {
    console.log('Stopped observing cart.totalPrice');
});

const disposer = autorun(() => {
    console.log(obj.get(), `Cart total: ${cart.totalPrice}`);
});
setTimeout(disposer);

obj.set(20);
cart.totalPrice = 100;
```

In the preceding snippet, the onBecomeObserved() handlers will be called when autorun() executes for the first time. Upon calling the disposer function, the onBecomeUnobserved() handlers are invoked. This can be seen in the following console output:

```
Started observing obj
Started observing cart.totalPrice
10 "Cart total: 0"
20 "Cart total: 0"
20 "Cart total: 100"
Stopped observing cart.totalPrice
Stopped observing obj
```

onBecomeObserved() and onBecomeUnobserved() are great hooks to lazily set up (and tear down) an observable on its first use (and last use). This is useful in cases where there might be an expensive operation that is required to set the initial value of the observable. Such operations can be lazily performed by deferring until it is actually used somewhere.

Lazy loading the temperature

Let's take an example where we will lazy load the *temperature* for a city, but only when it is accessed. This can be done by modeling the observable property with the hooks for onBecomeObserved() and onBecomeUnobserved(). The following snippet shows this in action:

```
// A mock service to simulate a network call to a weather API
const temperatureService = {
    fetch(location) {
        console.log('Invoked temperature-fetch');

        return new Promise(resolve =>
            setTimeout(resolve(Math.round(Math.random() * 35)), 200),
        );
    },
};

class City {
    @observable temperature;
    @observable location;

    interval;
    disposers;

    constructor(location) {
```

```
        this.location = location;
        const disposer1 = onBecomeObserved(
            this,
            'temperature',
            this.onActivated,
        );
        const disposer2 = onBecomeUnobserved(
            this,
            'temperature',
            this.onDeactivated,
        );

        this.disposers = [disposer1, disposer2];
    }

    onActivated = () => {
        this.interval = setInterval(() => this.fetchTemperature(), 5000);
        console.log('Temperature activated');
    };

    onDeactivated = () => {
        console.log('Temperature deactivated');
        this.temperature = undefined;
        clearInterval(this.interval);
    };

    fetchTemperature = flow(function*() {
        this.temperature = yield temperatureService.fetch(this.location);
    });

    cleanup() {
        this.disposers.forEach(disposer => disposer());
        this.disposers = undefined;
    }
}

const city = new City('Bengaluru');
const disposer = autorun(() =>
    console.log(`Temperature in ${city.location} is ${city.temperature}ºC`),
);

setTimeout(disposer, 15000);
```

The preceding console output shows you the activation and deactivation for the `temperature` observable. It is activated in `autorun()` and after 15 seconds, it gets *deactivated*. We kick off the timer that keeps updating the *temperature* in the `onBecomeObserved()` handler and clear it in the `onBecomeUnobserved()` handler. The *timer* is the resource we manage that is created only when the `temperature` is accessed and not before:

```
Temperature activated
Temperature in Bengaluru is undefined°C

Invoked temperature-fetch
Temperature in Bengaluru is 22°C
Invoked temperature-fetch
Temperature in Bengaluru is 32°C
Invoked temperature-fetch
Temperature in Bengaluru is 4°C

Temperature deactivated
```

Gatekeeper of changes

The changes you make to an observable are not applied immediately by MobX. Instead, they go through a layer of interceptors that have the ability to keep the change, modify it, or even discard it completely. This is all possible with the `intercept()` API. The signature is very similar to `onBecomeObserved` and `onBecomeUnobserved`, with the callback function (*interceptor*) giving you the change object:

```
disposer = intercept(observable, property?, interceptor: (change) =>
                        change | null )
```

`observable`: A boxed observable or an observable object/array/map.

`property`: The optional string name of the property you want to intercept on the observable. As we saw earlier for `onBecomeObserved` and `onBecomeUnobserved`, there is a difference between `intercept(cart, 'totalPrice', (change) => {})` and `intercept(cart.totalPrice, () => {})`. For the latter (`cart.totalPrice`), you are intercepting a value instead of the observable property. MobX will throw an error, stating that you haven't passed the correct type.

`interceptor`: A callback that receives the change object and is expected to return the final change; apply as-is, modify, or discard (`null`). It is also valid to throw an error in the interceptor to notify exceptional updates.

`disposer`: Gives back a function, which when called will cancel this interceptor. This is very similar to what we have seen with `onBecomeObserved()`, `onBecomeUnobserved()`, and even reactions like `autorun()`, `reaction()`, and `when()`.

Intercepting the change

The change argument that is received has some known fields that give the details. The most important of these are the `type` field, which tells you the *type of change*, and `object`, which gives the *object on which the change happened*. Depending upon the `type`, a few other fields add more context to the change:

- `type`: Can be one of add, delete, or update
- `object`: A boxed observable or the observable object/array/map instance
- `newValue`: When the type is add or update, this fields contains the new value
- `oldValue`: When the type is delete or update, this field carries the previous value

Inside the interceptor callback, you have the opportunity to finalize the type of change you actually want to apply. You can do one of the following:

- Return null and discard the change
- Update with a different value
- Throw an error indicating an exceptional value
- Return as-is and apply the change

Let's take an example of intercepting the theme changes and ensuring that only valid updates are applied. In the following snippet, you can see how we intercept the `color` property of the theme observable. The color can either be *light* or *dark*, or have a shorthand value of `1` or `d`. For any other value, we throw an error. We also guard against unsetting the color by returning `null` and discarding the change:

```
import { intercept, observable } from 'mobx';

const theme = observable({
    color: 'light',
    shades: [],
});

const disposer = intercept(theme, 'color', change => {
    console.log('Intercepting:', change);

    // Cannot unset value, so discard this change
    if (!change.newValue) {
```

```
            return null;
    }

    // Handle shorthand values
    const newTheme = change.newValue.toLowerCase();
    if (newTheme === 'l' || newTheme === 'd') {
        change.newValue = newTheme === 'l' ? 'light' : 'dark'; // set
          the correct value
        return change;
    }

    // check for a valid theme
    const allowedThemes = ['light', 'dark'];
    const isAllowed = allowedThemes.includes(newTheme);
    if (!isAllowed) {
        throw new Error(`${change.newValue} is not a valid theme`);
    }

    return change; // Correct value so return as-is
});
```

observe() the changes

The utility that acts as the counterpart of intercept() is observe(). observe(), as the name suggests, allows you to make granular observations on observables:

```
observe(observable, property?, observer: (change) => {})
```

The signature is exactly like intercept(), but the behavior is quite different. observe() is invoked *after the change* has been applied to the observable.

An interesting characteristic is that observe() is immune to *transactions*. What this means is that the *observer callback* is invoked immediately after a mutation and does not wait until the transaction completes. As you are aware, *actions* are the places where a mutation happens. MobX optimizes the notifications by firing them, but only after the top-most *action* completes. With observe(), you get an unfiltered view of the mutations as and when they happen.

 It is recommended to use autorun() whenever you feel a need for observe(). Use it only when you think you need immediate notification for a mutation.

The following example shows the various details you can observe on mutating an observable. As you can see, the change argument is exactly like intercept():

```js
import { observe, observable } from 'mobx';

const theme = observable({
    color: 'light',
    shades: [],
});

const disposer = observe(theme, 'color', change => {
    console.log(
        `Observing ${change.type}`,
        change.oldValue,
        '-->',
        change.newValue,
        'on',
        change.object,
    );
});

theme.color = 'dark';
```

Development utilities

As you scale your applications with more features, it becomes mandatory to understand how and when the MobX reactive system is being used. MobX comes with a set of debugging utilities that help you monitor and trace the various activities happening inside it. These give you a real-time view of all the observable changes, actions, and reactions firing inside the system.

Using spy() to track the reactivity

Earlier, we saw the observe() function, which allows you to *"observe"* the changes happening to a single observable. But what if you wanted to observe changes happening across all observables without having to individually set up the observe() handlers? That is where spy() comes in. It gives you insight into how the various observables in your system are changing over time:

```js
disposer = spy(listener: (event) => { })
```

It takes in a *listener function* that receives an event object carrying all the details. The *event* has properties very similar to the `observe()` handler. There is a `type` field that tells you about the type of the event. The type can be one of:

- **update**: For object, array, map
- **add**: For object, array, map
- **delete**: For map
- **create**: For boxed observables
- **action**: When an action fires
- **reaction**: Upon execution of `autorun()`, `reaction()`, or `when()`
- **compute**: For computed properties
- **error**: In case of any caught exceptions inside actions or reactions

Here is a snippet of code that sets up a `spy()` and prints the output to the console. We are also disposing this spy after five seconds:

```
import { spy } from 'mobx';

const disposer = spy(event => console.log(event));

setTimeout(disposer, 5000);

// Console output
{type: "action", name: "<unnamed action>", object: undefined, arguments:
Array(0), spyReportStart: true}
{type: "update", object: BookSearchStore, oldValue: 0, name:
"BookSearchStore@1", newValue: 2179, ...}
{spyReportEnd: true}
{object: Proxy, type: "splice", index: 0, removed: Array(0), added:
Array(20), ...}
{spyReportEnd: true}
{type: "update", object: BookSearchStore, oldValue: Proxy, name:
"BookSearchStore@1", newValue: Proxy, ...}
{spyReportEnd: true}
{type: "update", object: BookSearchStore, oldValue: "pending", name:
"BookSearchStore@1", newValue: "completed", ...}
```

Some of the spy events may be accompanied by `spyReportStart` or `spyReportEnd` properties. These mark a group of events that are related.

Using spy() directly is probably not your best option during development. It is better to rely on the visual debugger (discussed in the following section), which makes use of spy() to give you more readable logs. Note that the calls to spy() are a *no-op* for production builds when you set the NODE_ENV environment variable to *"production"*.

Tracing a reaction

While spy() gives you a lens to observe all changes happening in MobX, trace() is a utility that is specifically focused on computed properties, reactions, and component renders. You can find out why a *computed property, reaction,* or a *component render* is being invoked by simply placing a trace() statement inside it:

```
trace(thing?, property?, enterDebugger?)
```

It has three *optional* arguments:

- thing: An observable
- property: An observable property
- enterDebugger: A Boolean flag indicating whether you want to step into the debugger automatically

It is quite common to invoke a trace with: trace(true), which will pause inside the debugger upon invocation. For the book search example (from Chapter 3, *A React App with MobX*), we can place a trace statement right inside the render() of the SearchTextField component:

```
import { trace } from 'mobx';

@inject('store')
@observer
export class SearchTextField extends React.Component {
    render() {
        trace(true);
        /* ... */
    }

}
```

When the debugger is paused, you get a complete root-cause analysis of why this computed property, reaction, or render got executed. Inside the Chrome devtools, you can see these details like so:

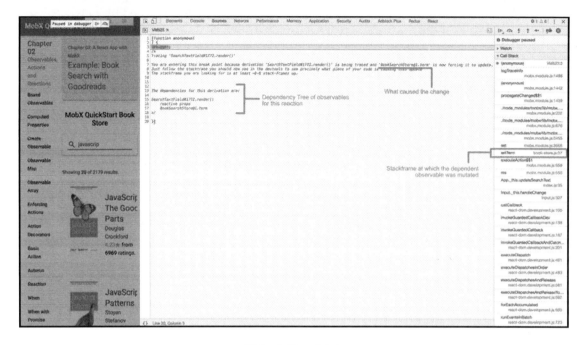

Details on the Chrome devtools

Visual debugging with mobx-react-devtools

`spy()` and `trace()` are great for getting a code-level insight into the MobX reactive system. However, when starting out your analysis of improving performance, visual debugging is quite handy. MobX has a sister NPM package called `mobx-react-devtools`, which gives you a simple `<DevTools />` component that can help you visualize how your component tree reacts to the observables. By including this component at the top of your app, you will see a toolbar at runtime:

```
import DevTools from 'mobx-react-devtools';
import React from 'react';

export class MobXBookApp extends React.Component {
    render() {
        return (
            <Fragment>
```

```
        <DevTools />
        <RootAppComponent />
    </Fragment>
);
    }
}
```

The screenshot below shows the MobX DevTools toolbar showing up in the *top-right* corner of the screen.

By enabling the buttons, you can see which components render upon changes in observables, see the dependency tree of observables connected to a DOM element, and print console logs whenever an *action/reaction* executes. Components will flash with a colored rectangle whenever they render. The color of the rectangle is an indication of how long it takes to render, *green* being the fastest and *red* being the slowest. You can observe the flashing rectangles to ensure that only the parts you intended to change are re-rendering. This is a great way to identify components that are rendering unnecessarily and possibly make more granular observers.

The `mobx-react-devtools` package relies on `spy()` to print the console logs for executing actions and reactions.

A few other APIs

There are some miscellaneous APIs that are provided by MobX that are not that frequently used. It is still worth mentioning them here for the sake of completeness.

Querying the reactive system

When dealing with the various abstractions in MobX (observables, actions, reactions), it is sometimes useful to know if a certain object, function, or value is of a certain kind. MobX has a set of *isXXX* APIs that help you to determine the type of the value:

- `isObservableObject(thing)`, `isObservableArray(thing)`, `isObservableMap(thing)`: Tells you whether the passed in value is an observable object, array, or map
- `isObservable(thing)` and `isObservableProp(thing, property?)`: Similar to the preceding point but more generalized check for an observable value
- `isBoxedObservable(thing)`: Whether the value is a boxed observable
- `isAction(func)`: Returns `true` if the function is wrapped by an action
- `isComputed(thing)` and `isComputedProp(thing, property?)`: Checks whether the value is a computed property

Probing deeper into the reactive system

MobX builds up a reactive fabric internally that keeps all of the observables and reactions connected. We will be exploring these internals in Chapter 9, *Mobx Internals*, where we will see the mention of certain terms like *atoms*. For now, let's take a quick look at the APIs that give you the internal representation of the observables and reactions:

- getAtom(thing, property?): At the heart of every observable is an Atom, which keeps track of the observers that depend on the observable value. Its purpose is to report whenever anyone reads or writes to the observable value. With this API, you get the instance of the Atom that backs the observable.
- getDependencyTree(thing, property?): This gives you the tree of dependencies that the given thing depends on. It can be used to get the dependencies for a computed property or a reaction.
- getObserverTree(thing, property?): This is a counterpart of getDependencyTree(), which gives you the observers that depend on the given thing.

Summary

Although there is a lean outer-level API for MobX, there is also a set of APIs for more fine-grained observation and mutation. We saw how the Object API can be used to make very surgical changes in your observable tree. With observe() and intercept(), you can track the changes happening in an observable and also intercept to modify the change.

spy() and trace() are your friends during debugging, and coupled with *mobx-react-devtools*, you have a visual debugger for identifying and improving render performance. These tools and utilities give you a rich Developer eXperience (DX) when working with MobX.

In Chapter 8, *Exploring mobx-utils and mobx-state-tree*, we will raise the bar on using MobX with the special packages mobx-utils and mobx-state-tree.

Exploring mobx-utils and mobx-state-tree

8

As you start going deeper into the world of MobX, you will realize that certain types of use cases recur quite often. The first time you solve them, there is a definite sense of achievement. However, after the fifth time, you want to standardize the solution. `mobx-utils` is an NPM package that gives you several standard utilities to handle common use cases in MobX.

To push the level of standardization even further, we can bring more structured opinions into our MobX solutions. These opinions have been formed out of several years of MobX usage, and carry a variety of ideas for rapid development. This is all possible with the `mobx-state-tree` NPM package.

In this chapter, we will cover the following packages in greater detail:

- `mobx-utils` for a tool belt of utility functions
- `mobx-state-tree` (**MST**) for an opinionated MobX

Technical requirements

You will be required to have Node.js installed on a system. Finally, to use the Git repository of this book, the user needs to install Git.

The code files of this chapter can be found on GitHub:
`https://github.com/PacktPublishing/Mobx-Quick-Start-Guide/tree/master/src/Chapter08`

Check out the following video to see the code in action:
`http://bit.ly/2LiFSJO`

The utility functions of mobx-utils

`mobx-utils` provides a variety of utility functions that can simplify programming tasks in MobX. You can install `mobx-utils` using `npm` or `yarn`:

```
$ npm install mobx-utils
```

In the rest of this section, we will focus on some utilities that are frequently used. These include the following:

- `fromPromise()`
- `lazyObservable()`
- `fromResource()`
- `now()`
- `createViewModel()`

Visualizing async-operations with fromPromise()

Promises, a way of life in JavaScript, are great for dealing with asynchronous operations. When representing the state of operations on the React UI, we have to ensure each of the three states of a promise is handled. This includes the state when the promise is `pending` (operation in progress), `fulfilled` (operation completed successfully), or `rejected` (in case of failures). `fromPromise()` is a convenient way to handle a promise, and gives a nice API to visually represent the three states:

```
newPromise = fromPromise(promiseLike)
```

`promiseLike`: instance of `Promise` or `(resolve, reject) => { }`

`fromPromise()` wraps the given promise and gives back a new, MobX-charged promise with some additional observable properties:

- `state`: One of the three string values: `pending`, `fulfilled`, or `rejected`: These are also available as constants on the `mobx-utils` package: `mobxUtils.PENDING`, `mobxUtils.FULFILLED`, and `mobxUtils.REJECTED`.
- `value`: The resolved `value` or the `rejected` error. Use `state` to distinguish the value.
- `case({pending, fulfilled, rejected})`: This is used to provide the React components for the three states.

Let's see all of this in action with an example. We will create a simple `Worker` class that performs some operation, which can randomly fail. Here is the `Worker` class that tracks the operation by calling `fromPromise()`. Notice that we are passing a `promise` as argument into `fromPromise()`:

```
import { fromPromise, PENDING, FULFILLED, REJECTED } from 'mobx-utils';
class Worker {
    operation = null;
    start() {
        this.operation = fromPromise(this.performOperation());
    }
    performOperation() {
        return new Promise((resolve, reject) => {
            const timeoutId = setTimeout(() => {
                clearTimeout(timeoutId);
                Math.random() > 0.25
                    ? resolve('200 OK')
                    : reject(new Error('500 FAIL'));
            }, 1000);
        });
    }
}
```

To visualize this operation, we can leverage the `case()` API to show the corresponding React component for each state. This can be seen in the following code. As the operation progresses from `pending` to `fulfilled` or `rejected`, these states will be rendered with the correct React component. For the `fulfilled` and `rejected` states, the resolved `value` or the `rejected error` is passed in as the first argument:

```
import { fromPromise, PENDING, FULFILLED, REJECTED } from 'mobx-utils';
import { observer } from 'mobx-react';

import React, { Fragment } from 'react';
import { CircularProgress, Typography } from '@material-ui/core/es/index';

@observer
export class FromPromiseExample extends React.Component {
    worker;

    constructor(props) {
        super(props);

        this.worker = new Worker();
        this.worker.start();
    }

    render() {
```

```
            const { operation } = this.worker;
            return operation.case({
                [PENDING]: () => (
                    <Fragment>
                        <CircularProgress size={50} color={'primary'} />
                        <Typography variant={'title'}>
                            Operation in Progress
                        </Typography>
                    </Fragment>
                ),
                [FULFILLED]: value => (
                    <Typography variant={'title'} color={'primary'}>
                        Operation completed with result: {value}
                    </Typography>
                ),
                [REJECTED]: error => (
                    <Typography variant={'title'} color={'error'}>
                        Operation failed with error: {error.message}
                    </Typography>
                ),
            });
        }
    }
```

 Instead of the `case()` function, we could have also switched manually on the observable `state` property. In fact, `case()` does that internally.

Using lazyObservable() for deferred updates

For operations that are expensive to perform, it makes sense to defer them until needed. With `lazyObservable()`, you can track the result of these operations and update only when needed. It takes in a function that performs the computation and pushes values when ready:

```
result = lazyObservable(sink => { }, initialValue)
```

Here, `sink` is the callback to be invoked to push the value onto `lazyObservable`. The lazy-observable can also start with some `initialValue`.

The current value of `lazyObservable()` can be retrieved using `result.current()`. Once a lazy-observable has been updated, `result.current()` will have some value. To update the lazy-observable again, you can use `result.refresh()`. This will re-invoke the computation and eventually push new values via the `sink` callback. Note that the `sink` callback can be invoked as many times as needed.

In the following snippet, you can see the use of `lazyObservable()` to update the value of the operation:

```
import { lazyObservable } from 'mobx-utils';

class ExpensiveWorker {
    operation = null;

    constructor() {
        this.operation = lazyObservable(async sink => {
            sink(null); // push an empty value before the update
            const result = await this.performOperation();
            sink(result);
        });
    }

    performOperation() {
        return new Promise(resolve => {
            const timeoutId = setTimeout(() => {
                clearTimeout(timeoutId);
                resolve('200 OK');
            }, 1000);
        });
    }
}
```

 The call to the `current()` method is tracked by MobX, so make sure you only call it when needed. The use of this method inside `render()` causes MobX to re-render the component. After all, `render()` of a component translates to a reaction in MobX, which re-evaluates whenever any of its tracked observables change.

To use the lazy-observable inside a React component (an *observer*), we rely on the `current()` method to fetch its value. MobX will track this value and re-render the component whenever it changes. Notice in the `onClick` handler of the button, we are causing an update of the lazy-observable by calling its `refresh()` method:

```
import { observer } from 'mobx-react';
import React, { Fragment } from 'react';
import {
```

```
    Button,
    CircularProgress,
    Typography,
} from '@material-ui/core/es/index';

@observer
export class LazyObservableExample extends React.Component {
    worker;
    constructor(props) {
        super(props);

        this.worker = new ExpensiveWorker();
    }
    render() {
        const { operation } = this.worker;
        const result = operation.current();
        if (!result) {
            return (
                <Fragment>
                    <CircularProgress size={50} color={'primary'} />
                    <Typography variant={'title'}>
                        Operation in Progress
                    </Typography>
                </Fragment>
            );
        }
        return (
            <Fragment>
                <Typography variant={'title'} color={'primary'}>
                    Operation completed with result: {result}
                </Typography>
                <Button
                    variant={'raised'}
                    color={'primary'}
                    onClick={() => operation.refresh()}
                >
                    Redo Operation
                </Button>
            </Fragment>
        );
    }
}
```

A generalized lazyObservable() with fromResource()

There is also a more generalized form of `lazyObservable()` called `fromResource()`. Similar to `lazyResource()`, it takes in a function with the `sink` callback. This acts as a *subscribing* function, which is invoked only when the resource is actually requested. Additionally, it takes a second argument, an *unsubscribing* function, which can be used to clean up when the resource is no longer needed:

```
resource = fromResource(subscriber: sink => {}, unsubscriber: () => {},
            initialValue)
```

`fromResource()` gives back an observable which will start fetching values when its `current()` method is invoked the first time. It gives back an observable that also has the `dispose()` method to stop updating values.

In the following snippet, you can see a `DataService` class relying on `fromResource()` to manage its WebSocket connection. The value of the data can be retrieved with `data.current()`. Here, *data* acts as the lazy-observable. In the *subscribing* function, we set up our WebSocket and subscribe to a specific channel. We unsubscribe from this channel in the *unsubscribing* function of `fromResource()`:

```
import { fromResource } from 'mobx-utils';

class DataService {
    data = null;
    socket = null;

    constructor() {
        this.data = fromResource(
            async sink => {
                this.socket = new WebSocketConnection();
                await this.socket.subscribe('data');

                const result = await this.socket.get();

                sink(result);
            },
            () => {
                this.socket.unsubscribe('data');
                this.socket = null;
            },
        );
    }
}

const service = new DataService();
```

```
console.log(service.data.current());

// After some time, when no longer needed
service.data.dispose();
```

We can explicitly dispose of the resource with the `dispose()` method. However, MobX is smart enough to know when there are no more observers of this resource and automatically calls the *unsubscribe* function.

 A special kind of lazy-observable provided by `mobx-utils` is `now(interval: number)`. It treats time as an observable and updates at the given interval. You can retrieve its value by simply calling `now()`, which, by default, updates every second. By the virtue of being an observable, it will also cause any reaction to execute every second. Internally, `now()` uses the `fromResource()` utility to manage the timer.

A view model to manage edits

In a data-entry-based application, it is quite common to have forms to accept a variety of fields. In these forms, the original model is not mutated until the user submits the form. This allows the user to cancel out of the editing process and go back to the previous values. A scenario like this requires creating a clone of the original model and pushing the edits upon submit. Although this technique is not terribly complex, it does add some boilerplate.

`mobx-utils` provides a handy utility called `createViewModel()` that is tailor-made for this scenario:

```
viewModel = createViewModel(model)
```

`model` is the original model containing observable properties. `createViewModel()` wraps this model and proxies all the reads and writes. This utility has some interesting characteristics, as follows:

- As long as a property of `viewModel` is not changed, it will return the value from the original model. After a change, it will return the updated value and also treat `viewModel` as dirty.
- To finalize the updated values on the original model, you must call the `submit()` method of `viewModel`. To reverse any changes, you can invoke the `reset()` method. To revert a single property, use `resetProperty(propertyName: string)`.

- To check if `viewModel` is dirty, use the `isDirty` property. To check if a single property is dirty, use `isPropertyDirty(propertyName: string)`.
- To get the original model, use the handy `model()` method.

The advantage of using `createViewModel()` is that you can treat the whole editing process as a single transaction. It is final only when `submit()` is invoked. This allows you to cancel out prematurely and retain the original model in its previous state.

In the following example, we are creating a `viewModel` that wraps the `FormData` instance and logs the `viewModel` and `model` properties. You will notice the proxying effect of `viewModel` and how values propagate back to the model upon `submit()`:

```
class FormData {
    @observable name = '<Unnamed>';
    @observable email = '';
    @observable favoriteColor = '';
}

const viewModel = createViewModel(new FormData());

autorun(() => {
    console.log(
        `ViewModel: ${viewModel.name}, Model: ${
            viewModel.model.name
        }, Dirty: ${viewModel.isDirty}`,
    );
});

viewModel.name = 'Pavan';
viewModel.email = 'pavan@pixelingene.com';
viewModel.favoriteColor = 'orange';

console.log('About to reset');
viewModel.reset();

viewModel.name = 'MobX';

console.log('About to submit');
viewModel.submit();
```

The log from `autorun()` is as follows. You can see the effect of `submit()` and `reset()` on the `viewModel.name` property:

```
ViewModel: <Unnamed>, Model: <Unnamed>, Dirty: false
ViewModel: Pavan, Model: <Unnamed>, Dirty: true
About to reset...
ViewModel: <Unnamed>, Model: <Unnamed>, Dirty: false
ViewModel: MobX, Model: <Unnamed>, Dirty: true
About to submit...
ViewModel: MobX, Model: MobX, Dirty: false
```

There is lot more to discover

The handful of utilities described here is by no means exhaustive. `mobx-utils` provides many more utilities, and we strongly encourage you to take a look at the GitHub project (`https://github.com/mobxjs/mobx-utils`) to discover the remaining utility functions.

There are functions to convert between RxJS streams and MobX Observables, *processor-functions* that can perform an operation anytime an observable-array is appended, a variant of the MobX `when()`, which automatically disposes after a timeout, and many more.

An opinionated MobX with mobx-state-tree

MobX is very flexible in how you organize your state and apply the various actions and reactions. However, it does leave some questions for you to answer:

- Should classes be used or just plain objects with `extendObservable()`?
- How should the data be normalized?
- How to deal with circular references when serializing the state?
- And many more

`mobx-state-tree` is a package that gives you prescriptive guidance for organizing and structuring your observable state. Adopting the MST style of thinking gives you several benefits out of the box. In this section, we will explore this package and its benefits.

Models – properties, views, and actions

mobx-state-tree as the name suggests, organizes the state in a tree of models. It's a model-first approach, where each model defines the state that needs to be captured. Defining the model adds the ability to type-check the model assignments at runtime and guard you against inadvertent changes. Combining the runtime checks with the use of a language like TypeScript also gets you compile-time (or rather, design-time) type-safety. With a strictly typed model, mobx-state-tree gives you safe guarantees and ensures the integrity and constraints of your typed-models. This in itself is a huge benefit, especially when dealing with a dynamic language like JavaScript.

Let's put MST into action with a simple model for Todo:

```
import { types } from 'mobx-state-tree';

const Todo = types.model('Todo', {
    title: types.string,
    done: false,
});
```

A model describes the shape of data it holds. In case of the Todo model, it only needs a title *string* and a *boolean* done property. Note that we assigned our model to a capitalized name (Todo). This is because MST really defines a type and not an instance.

All of the built-in types in MST are part of the types namespace. The types.model() method takes two arguments: an optional string *name* (used for debugging and error reporting) and an *object* defining the various properties of the type. All of these properties will be qualified with strict types. Let's try creating an instance of this model:

```
const todo = Todo.create({
    title: 'Read a book',
    done: false,
});
```

Notice how we have passed the same structure of data into Todo.create() as defined in the model. Passing any other kind of data will result in MST throwing type-errors. Creating an instance of the model has also made all its properties into observables. This means we can now use the full power of the MobX API.

Let's create a simple reaction that will log the changes to the `todo` instance:

```
import { autorun } from 'mobx';

autorun(() => {
    console.log(`${todo.title}: ${todo.done}`);
});

// Toggle the done flag
todo.done = !todo.done;
```

If you run this code, you will notice an exception being thrown, as follows:

```
Error: [mobx-state-tree] Cannot modify 'Todo@<root>', the object is
protected and can only be modified by using an action.
```

This happens because we have modified the `todo.done` property outside of an action. You will recollect from earlier chapters that it's a good practice to wrap all observable-mutations inside an action. In fact, there is even a MobX API: `configure({ enforceActions: 'strict' })`, to ensure this happens. MST is very *protective* about the data in its state-tree and mandates the use of actions for all mutations.

This may sound very rigid, but it does come with added benefits. For example, the use of actions allows MST to provide first-class support for middleware. Middleware can *intercept* any changes happening to the state-tree and make it trivial to implement features such as *Logging, Time Traveling, Undo/Redo, Database Synchronization*, and so on.

Defining actions on the model

The model type `Todo` that we created earlier can be extended with a chained API. `actions()` is one such API that can be used to extend the model type with all the action definitions. Let's do that for our `Todo` type:

```
const Todo = types
    .model('Todo', {
        title: types.string,
        done: false,
    })
    .actions(self => ({
        toggle() {
            self.done = !self.done;
        },
    }));

const todo = Todo.create({
```

```
        title: 'Read a book',
        done: false,
});

autorun(() => {
    console.log(`${todo.title}: ${todo.done}`);
});

todo.toggle();
```

The `actions()` method takes in a function that receives the instance of the model as its argument. Here, we are calling it `self`. This function is supposed to return a key-value map that defines all the actions. In the preceding snippet, we are leveraging the object-literal syntax of ES2015 to make the actions object look more readable. There are some striking benefits of this style of accepting the actions:

- The use of a function allows you to create a closure that can be used to track the private state that is only used by the actions. For example, a WebSocket connection that is set up inside one of the actions that should never be exposed to the outside world.
- By passing an instance of the model to `actions()`, you can guarantee that the `this` pointer is always correct. You never have to worry about the context of the functions defined in `actions()` anymore. The `toggle()` action makes use of `self` to mutate the model instance.

The actions defined can be invoked directly on the model instance, which is what we do with `todo.toggle()`. MST has no more complaints about direct mutation, and `autorun()` will also fire when `todo.done` changes.

Creating derived information with views

Similar to actions, we can also extend the model type with `views()`. Derived information in a model is defined using `views()` in MST. Just like the `actions()` method, it can be chained to the model type:

```
const Todo = types
    .model(/* ... */)
    .actions(/* ... */)
    .views(self => ({
        get asMarkdown() {
            return self.done
                ? `* [x] ~~${self.title}~~`
                : `* [ ] ${self.title}`;
```

```
        },

        contains(text) {
            return self.title.indexOf(text) !== -1;
        },
    }));

const todo = Todo.create({
    title: 'Read a book',
    done: false,
});

autorun(() => {
    console.log(`Title contains "book"?: ${todo.contains('book')}`);
});

console.log(todo.asMarkdown);
// * [ ] Read a book

console.log(todo.contains('book')); // true
```

There are two views introduced on the `Todo` type:

- `asMarkdown()` is a *getter* that translates to a MobX computed-property. Like every computed-property, its output is cached.
- `contains()` is a regular function whose output is not cached. However, it does have the ability to re-execute when used in a reactive context such as `reaction()` or `autorun()`.

`mobx-state-tree` introduces a very strict concept of models with clearly defined *state*, *actions*, and *derivations*. If you feel uncertain about structuring your code in MobX, MST can help you apply the MobX philosophy with clear guidance.

Fine-tuning primitive types

The single model type that we have seen so far is just the beginning and can barely be called a tree. We can expand the domain-model to make it more realistic. Let's add a `User` type, who will be creating the `todo` items:

```
import { types } from 'mobx-state-tree';

const User = types.model('User', {
    name: types.string,
    age: 42,
```

```
        twitter: types.maybe(types.refinement(types.string, v =>
            /^\w+$/.test(v))),
    });
```

There are some interesting details in the preceding definition, as follows:

- The `age` property has been defined as the constant `42`, which translates to a default value for `age`. When no value is provided for a user, it will be set to this default value. Additionally, MST is smart enough to derive the type to be `number`. This works well for all the primitive types, where the type of the default value will be inferred as the type of the property. Also, by giving a default value, we are suggesting that the `age` property is optional. A more verbose form of declaring the property is: `types.optional(types.number, 42)`.

- The `twitter` property has a more complicated definition but can be broken down easily. `types.maybe()` suggests that a `twitter` handle is optional, so it could be *undefined*. When a value is provided, it must be of type string. But not any string; only strings that match the provided regular-expression. This gives you runtime type-safety and rejects invalid Twitter handles such as `Calvin & Hobbes` or an empty string.

The type system provided by MST is very powerful and can handle a variety of complex type specifications. It also composes well, and gives you a functional approach to combining many smaller types into a larger type definition. These type specifications give you runtime safety and ensure the integrity of your domain model.

Composing trees

Now that we have the `Todo` and `User` types, we can define the top-level `App` type that composes the types defined previously. The `App` type represents the state of the application:

```
const App = types.model('App', {
    todos: types.array(Todo),
    users: types.map(User),
});

const app = App.create({
    todos: [
        { title: 'Write the chapter', done: false },
        { title: 'Review the chapter', done: false },
    ],
    users: {
        michel: {
            name: 'Michel Westrate',
```

```
                twitter: 'mwestrate',
            },
            pavan: {
                name: 'Pavan Podila',
                twitter: 'pavanpodila',
            },
        },
    });

    app.todos[0].toggle();
```

We have defined the `App` type by using *higher-order types* (types that take a type as input and create a new type). In the preceding snippet, `types.map()` and `types.array()` create these higher-order types.

Creating an instance of the `App` type is just a matter of providing the right JSON payload. As long as the structure matches the type-specification, MST will have no problem in constructing the model instances at runtime.

Remember: The shape of the data will always be validated by MST. It will never allow data updates that don't match the model's type specification.

Notice in the preceding snippet, we are able to call the `app.todos[0].toggle()` method seamlessly. This is because MST was able to build the `app` instance successfully and wrap the JSON nodes with proper types.

`mobx-state-tree` elevates the importance of modeling your application state. Defining the proper types for the various entities in your application is paramount for its structural and data integrity. A nice way to get started is to encode the JSON you receive from the server in MST models. The next step is to *fatten* the model by adding more rigid typing, and attaching actions and views.

References and identifiers

So far, this chapter has been entirely about capturing the state of the application in a *tree*. Trees have many interesting properties and are easy to comprehend and explore. But often, when one starts to apply a new technology to real problem domains, it turns out that trees are conceptually not sufficient to describe problem domains. For example, *friendship-relationships* are bidirectional and don't fit unidirectional trees. Dealing with relationships that are not *compositional* in nature, but rather *associative*, often requires introducing new abstraction layers and techniques such as *data normalization*.

A quick example of such a relationship can be introduced in our application by giving `Todo` an `assignee` property. Now, it is clear that `Todo` does not *own* its `assignee`, and neither is the inverse true; *todos* are not owned by a single user, as they can be *reassigned* later. So when composition does not suffice to describe the relationship, we often fall back to using *foreign keys* to describe the relationships.

In other words, the JSON of a `Todo` item could be like the following code, where the `assignee` field of `Todo` corresponds to the `userid` field of a `User` object:

 Using `name` to store the `assignee` relationship would be a bad idea, as the `name` of a person is not unique and it might change over time.

```
{
    todos: [
        {
            title: 'Learn MST',
            done: false,
            assignee: '37',
        },
    ],
    users: {
        '37': {
            userid: '37',
            name: 'Michel Weststrate',
            age: 33,
            twitter: 'mweststrate',
        },
    },
}
```

Our initial take on this might be to type the `assignee` and `userid` attributes
as `types.string` fields. Then, whenever we need it, we could look up the designated user
in the `users` map, since the user is stored under its own `userid`. Since the user lookup
could be a commonly needed operation, we could even introduce a *view* and *action* to read
or write to that user. That will make our user model as seen in the following code:

```javascript
import { types, getRoot } from 'mobx-state-tree';

const User = types.model('User', {
    userid: types.string, // uniquely identifies this User
    name: types.string,
    age: 42,
    twitter: types.maybe(types.refinement(types.string, v =>
/^\w+$/.test(v))),
});

const Todo = types
    .model('Todo', {
        assignee: types.string, // represents a User
        title: types.string,
        done: false,
    })
    .views(self => ({
        getAssignee() {
            if (!this.assignee) return undefined;
            return getRoot(self).users.get(this.assignee);
        },
    }))
    .actions(self => ({
        setAssignee(user) {
            if (typeof user === 'string') this.assignee = user;
            else if (User.is(user)) this.assignee = user.userid;
            else throw new Error('Not a valid user object or user id');
        },
    }));

const App = {
    /* as is */
};

const app = App.create(/* ... */);

console.log(app.todos[0].getAssignee().name); // Michel Weststrate
```

In the `getAssignee()` view, we conveniently use the fact that every MST node knows its own location in the tree. By leveraging the `getRoot()` utility, we can navigate to the `users` map and grab the correct `User` object. By using the `getAssignee()` view, we obtain a real `User` object so that we can directly access and print its `name` property.

> There are several useful utilities that can be used to reflect on or work with the location in a tree, such as `getPath()`, `getParent()`, `getParentOfType()`, and so on. As an alternative, we could have expressed the `getAssignee()` view as `return resolvePath(self, "../../users/" + self.assignee)`.
>
> We can treat the MST tree as a filesystem for state! `getAssignee()` just translates to a symlink.

Additionally, an action to update the `assignee` property has been introduced. To make sure the `setAssignee()` action can be conveniently invoked by either providing `userid`, or an actual *user* object, we apply some *type-discrimination*. In MST, every type not only exposes the `create()` method, but also the `is` method, to check if a given value is of the respective type.

Referencing by types.identifier() and types.reference()

It is nice that we can neatly express these lookup/update utilities in MST, but if your problem domain is large, this becomes quite a repetitive pattern. Luckily, this pattern is built into MST. The first type we can leverage is `types.identifier()`, which indicates that a certain field uniquely identifies an instance of a certain model type. So, in our example, rather than typing `userid` as `types.string` we can type it as `types.identifier()`.

Secondly, there is `types.reference()`. This type indicates that a certain field is serialized as a primitive value, but actually denotes a reference to another type in the tree. MST will automatically match `identifier` fields with `reference` fields for us, so we can simplify our previous state-tree model to the following:

```
import { types } from "mobx-state-tree"

const User = types.model("User", {
  userid: types.identifier(), // uniquely identifies this User
  name: types.string,
  age: 42,
  twitter: types.maybe(types.refinement(types.string, (v =>
/^\w+$/.test(v))))
```

```
})

const Todo = types.model("Todo", {
  assignee: types.maybe(types.reference(User)), // a Todo can be assigned
to a User
  title: types.string,
  done: false
})

const App = /* as is */

const app = App.create(/* */)
console.log(app.todos[0].assignee.name) // Michel Weststrate
```

Thanks to the reference type, reading the `assignee` attribute of `Todo` will actually resolve the stored identifier and return the correct `User` object. Thus, we can immediately print its name in the preceding example. Note that, behind the scenes, our state is still a tree. It is also important to notice that we don't have to specify where or how references to `User` instances should be resolved. MST will automatically maintain an internal *type + identifier* based lookup table for resolving references. By using *references* and *identifiers*, MST has enough type information to automatically handle the *data (de)normalization* for us.

> `types.reference` is quite powerful and can be customized to, for example, resolve objects based on relative paths (like a real symlink!) instead of identifiers. In many cases, you will combine `types.reference` with `types.maybe` as above, to express that `Todo` does not necessarily have an `assignee`. Likewise, arrays and maps of references can be modeled in similar ways.

Out-of-the-box benefits of declarative models

MST helps you organize and model complex problem domains in a declarative fashion. Because of a consistent approach to defining the types in your domain, we get the benefit of a clean and simple mental model. This consistency also gets us many *out-of-the-box* features, since MST has deep knowledge of the state-tree. One example we saw earlier was with automatic *data-normalization* with the use of *identifiers* and *references*. There are many more features built into MST. Of the lot, a few stand out as being most practical. We will briefly discuss them in the rest of this section.

Immutable snapshots

MST always keeps an immutable version of the state-tree in memory, which can be retrieved using the getSnapshot() API. Essentially, const snapshot = getSnapshot(tree) is the inverse of const tree = Type.create(snapshot). getSnapshot() makes it very convenient to quickly serialize the entire state of a tree. Since MST is powered by MobX, we can nicely track this as well.

Snapshots translate to *computed-properties* on the model instances.

The following snippet automatically stores the state of the tree in *local-storage* upon each change, but no more than once per second:

```
import { reaction } from 'mobx';
import { getSnapshot } from 'mobx-state-tree';

const app = App.create(/* as before */);

reaction(
    () => getSnapshot(app),
    snapshot => {
        window.localStorage.setItem('app', JSON.stringify(snapshot));
    },
    { delay: 1000 },
);
```

It should be pointed out that every node in an MST tree is an MST tree in itself. This means, any operation invoked on the root could also be invoked on any of its subtrees. For example, if we only want to store a part of the entire state, we could just get a snapshot of the subtree.

A corollary API that goes hand in hand with getSnapshot() is applySnapshot(). This can be used to update a tree with a snapshot in an efficient manner. By combining getSnapshot() and applySnapshot(), you can build a time traveler in just a few lines of code! This is left as an exercise for the reader.

JSON patches

Although snapshots efficiently capture the state of the entire application, they are not suitable for frequent communication with a server or other clients. This is because the size of a snapshot grows linearly with the size of the state you want to serialize. Instead, for real-time changes, it is better to send incremental updates to the server. *JSON-patch* (RFC-6902) is an official standard on how these incremental updates should be serialized, and MST supports this standard out of the box.

The onPatch() API can be used to listen to the patches being generated as a side effect of your changes. On the other hand, applyPatch() performs the inverse process: given a patch, it can update an existing tree. The onPatch() listener emits the patches generated as a result of the state changes made by actions. It also exposes the so-called *inverse-patches*: a set that can undo the changes made by the patches:

```
import { onPatch } from 'mobx-state-tree';

const app = App.create(/* see above */);

onPatch(app, (patches, inversePatches) => {
    console.dir(patches, inversePatches);
});

app.todos[0].toggle();
```

The preceding code, which toggles the todo, prints the following to the console:

```
// patches:

[{
    op: "replace",
    path: "/todos/0/done",
    value: true
}]

// inverse-patches:

[{
    op: "replace",
    path: "/todos/0/done",
    value: false
}]
```

Middlewares

We briefly mentioned middlewares in an earlier section, but let's expand on it here. Middlewares act as interceptors of the actions invoked on the state-tree. Because MST mandates the use of actions, we are assured that every *action* will pass through the middleware. The presence of middleware makes it trivial to implement several cross-cutting features, such as the following:

- Logging
- Authentication
- Time travel
- Undo/Redo

In fact, the `mst-middlewares` NPM package contains some of the previously mentioned middlewares, as well as a few more. For more details about these middlewares, refer to: `https://github.com/mobxjs/mobx-state-tree/blob/master/packages/mst-middlewares/README.md`.

Further reading

We have hardly scratched the surface of MobX-State-Tree, but hopefully it has left an impression around organizing and structuring the observable state in MobX. It is a well-defined, community-driven approach that bakes in many of the best practices discussed throughout this book. For a deeper exploration of MST, you can refer to the official getting-started guide at: `https://github.com/mobxjs/mobx-state-tree/blob/master/docs/getting-started.md#getting-started`.

Summary

In this chapter, we covered the practical aspects of adopting MobX with packages such as `mobx-utils` and `mobx-state-tree`. These packages codify the community wisdom around using MobX for a variety of scenarios.

`mobx-utils` gives you a set of utilities for tackling asynchronous tasks, dealing with expensive updates, creating view models for transactional-editing, and much more.

`mobx-state-tree` is a comprehensive package that is meant to simplify application development with MobX. It takes a prescriptive approach to structuring and organizing the observable state in MobX. With such a declarative approach, MST is able to get a deeper understanding of the state-tree and offer a variety of features, such as runtime type-checking, snapshots, JSON-patches, middlewares, and so on. Overall, it helps in developing a crisp mental model of your MobX application and puts the typed-domain-model at the forefront.

In the next chapter, we will culminate the journey on MobX with a peek into its inner workings. If there are parts of MobX that seem like *black magic,* the next chapter will dispel all such myths.

9
Mobx Internals

The MobX we have seen so far was from a consumer's standpoint, which focused on how it should be used, the best practices, and the APIs for tackling real-world use cases. This chapter takes it a level below and exposes the machinery behind the MobX reactive system. We will look at the underpinnings and the core abstractions that makes the triad of *Observables-Actions-Reactions* come to life.

The topics that will be covered in this chapter include the following:

- The layered architecture of MobX
- Atoms and ObservableValues
- Derivations and reactions
- What is *Transparent Functional Reactive Programming*?

Technical requirements

You will be required to have Node.js installed on a system. Finally, to use the Git repository of this book, the user needs to install Git.

The code files of this chapter can be found on GitHub:
```
https://github.com/PacktPublishing/Mobx-Quick-Start-Guide/tree/master/src/
Chapter09
```

Check out the following video to see the code in action:
```
http://bit.ly/2LvAouE
```

A layered architecture

Like any good system, MobX is built up of layers where each layer provides the services and behaviors for the higher layers. If you apply this lens on MobX, you can see these layers, bottom-up:

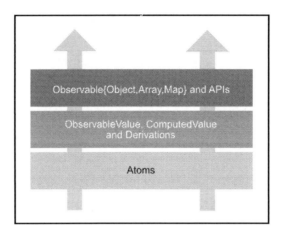

- **Atoms**: Atoms are the foundation of MobX observables. As the name suggests, they are the atomic pieces of the observable dependency tree. It keeps track of its observers but does not actually store any value.
- **ObservableValue, ComputedValue, and Derivations**: `ObservableValue` extends `Atom` and provides the actual storage. It is also the core implementation of boxed Observables. In parallel, we have derivations and reactions, which are the *observers* of the atoms. They respond to changes in atoms and schedule reactions. `ComputedValue` builds upon the derivations and also acts as an observable.
- **Observable{Object, Array, Map} and APIs**: These data structures build on top of `ObservableValue` and use it to represent their properties and values. This also acts as the API layer of MobX, the primary means of interfacing with the library from the consumer's standpoint.

 The separation of layers is also visible in the source code where there are separate folders for different abstraction layers of MobX. It is not a one-to-one match with what we have described here, but conceptually these layers have lot of parallels in code as well. All of the code in MobX has been written using TypeScript with first class support.

The Atom

The reactive system of MobX is backed by a graph of dependencies that exist between the observables. One observable's value could depend on a set of observables, which in turn could depend on other observables. For example, a shopping cart could have a *computed property* called `description` that depends on the array of `items` it holds and any `coupons` that were applied. Internally, `coupons` could depend on the `validCoupons` *computed property* of the `CouponManager` class. In code, this could look like so:

```
class Coupon {
    @observable isValid = false;

    /*...*/
}

class CouponManager {
    @observable.ref coupons = [];

    @computed
    get validCoupons() {
        return this.coupons.filter(coupon => coupon.isValid);
    }

    /*...*/
}

class ShoppingCart {
    @observable.shallow items = [];

    couponManager = new CouponManager();

    @computed
    get coupons() {
        return this.couponManager.validCoupons;
    }

    @computed
    get description() {
        return `Cart has ${this.items.length} item(s) with ${
            this.coupons.length
        } coupon(s) applied.`;
    }

    /*...*/
}
```

Visualizing this set of dependencies could give us a simple diagram like so:

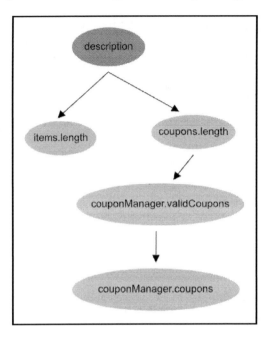

At runtime, MobX will create a backing dependency tree. Each node in this tree will be represented by an instance of Atom, the core building block of MobX. Thus, we can expect five *atoms* for the nodes in the tree in the preceding diagram.

An atom serves two purposes:

- Notify when it is *read*. This is done by calling reportObserved().
- Notify when it is *changed*. This is done by calling reportChanged().

 As a node of the MobX reactivity fabric, an atom plays the important role of notifying the reads and writes happening on each node.

Internally, an atom keeps track of its observers and informs them of the changes. This will happen when reportChanged() is called. A glaring omission here is that the actual value of the atom is not stored in the Atom itself. For that, we have a subclass called ObservableValue that builds on top of the Atom. We will look at that in the next section.

So, an atom's core contract consists of the two methods we mentioned earlier. It also contains a few housekeeping properties like an array of `observers`, whether it is being observed, and so on. We can safely ignore them for our discussion:

```
class Atom {
    observers = [];

    reportObserved() {}
    reportChanged() {}

    /* ... */
}
```

Reading atoms at runtime

MobX also gives you the ability to see the backing atoms at runtime. Going back to our previous example of the computed `description` property, let's explore its dependency tree:

```
import { autorun, $mobx, getDependencyTree } from 'mobx';

const cart = new ShoppingCart();
const disposer = autorun(() => {
    console.log(cart.description);
});

const descriptionAtom = cart[$mobx].values.get('description');
console.log(getDependencyTree(descriptionAtom));
```

There are few details that stand out in the preceding snippet:

- MobX gives you a special symbol, `$mobx`, that contains a reference to the internal housekeeping structure of the observable. The `cart` instance maintains a map of all of its observable properties using `cart[$mobx].values`. The backing atom for the `description` property is obtained by reading from this map: `cart[$mobx].values.get('description')`.
- We can get hold of the dependency tree for this property using the `getDependencyTree()` function exposed by MobX. It takes in an `Atom` as its input and gives back an object describing the dependency tree.

Here is the output of `getDependencyTree()` for the `description` property. A few extra details have been removed for clarity. The reason why you see `ShoppingCart@16.items` mentioned twice is because it points to the `items` (the reference) and `items.length` properties:

```
{
    name: 'ShoppingCart@16.description',
    dependencies: [
        { name: 'ShoppingCart@16.items' },
        { name: 'ShoppingCart@16.items' },
        {
            name: 'ShoppingCart@16.coupons',
            dependencies: [
                {
                    name: 'CouponManager@19.validCoupons',
                    dependencies: [{ name: 'CouponManager@19.coupons' }],
                },
            ],
        },
    ],
};
```

There is also a convenient API, `getAtom(thing: any, property: string)`, to read atoms from observables and observers. For example, in our previous example, instead of using the special symbol `$mobx` and reading into its internal structure, we can get the *description* atom with `getAtom(cart, 'description')`. `getAtom()` is exported from the `mobx` package.

As an exercise, find out the dependency tree for `autorun()` in the previous code snippet. You can get hold of the instance of the reaction with `disposer[$mobx]` or `getAtom(disposer)`. Similarly, there is also the `getObserverTree()` utility that gives you the observers depending on the given observable. See if you can find the connection to `autorun()` from the atom backing the `description` property.

Creating an Atom

As a MobX user, you would rarely use an `Atom` directly. Instead, you would rely on other convenience APIs exposed by MobX or data structures like `ObservableObject`, `ObservableArray`, or `ObservableMap`. However, the real world always creates situations where you may have to dive a few levels deeper.

MobX does give you a convenient factory function for creating atoms, aptly named
`createAtom()`:

```
createAtom(name, onBecomeObservedHandler, onBecomeUnobservedHandler)
```

- `name` (`string`): The name of the atom, which is utilized by the debugging and tracing facilities in MobX
- `onBecomeObservedHandler` (`() => { }`): A callback function to get notified when an atom gets observed for the first time
- `onBecomeUnobservedHandler` (`() => { }`): A callback function to get notified when an atom is no longer being observed

`onBecomeObserved` and `onBecomeUnobserved` are the two points in time when an atom becomes active and inactive in the reactivity system. These are normally meant for resource management, to set up and tear down, respectively.

The atomic clock example

Let's look at an example of using `Atom` that also illustrates how an atom participates in the reactive system. We will create a *simple clock* that starts ticking when an atom gets observed and stops when it is no longer observed. In essence, our resource here is the timer (clock) that is being managed by the use of an `Atom`:

```
import { createAtom, autorun } from 'mobx';

class Clock {

    constructor() {
        this.atom = createAtom(
            'Clock',
            () => {
                this.startTicking();
            },
            () => {
                this.stopTicking();
            },
        );

        this.intervalId = null;
    }

    startTicking() {
        console.log('Clock started');
```

```
        this.tick();
        this.intervalId = setInterval(() => this.tick(), 1000);
    }

    stopTicking() {
        clearInterval(this.intervalId);
        this.intervalId = null;

        console.log('Clock stopped');
    }

    tick() {
        this.atom.reportChanged();
    }

    get() {
        this.atom.reportObserved();
        return new Date();
    }
}

const clock = new Clock();

const disposer = autorun(() => {
    console.log(clock.get());
});

setTimeout(disposer, 3000);
```

There are many interesting details in the preceding snippet. Let's list them out here:

- In the call to `createAtom()`, we are supplying the handler when the atom becomes observed and also when it is no longer being observed. It might seem a little mysterious when the ato*m actually becomes observed*. The secret here is the use of `autorun()`, which sets up a side effect to read the current value of the atomic clock. S*ince an* `autorun()` runs immediately, `clock.get()` is called, which in turn calls `this.atom.reportObserved()`. This is how the atom becomes active in the reactive system.
- Once the atom becomes observed, we start the clock timer, which ticks every second. This is happening in the `onBecomeObserved` callback, where we call `this.startTicking()`.
- Every second, we call `this.atom.reportChanged()`, which propagates the changed value to all observers. In our case, we only have one, `autorun()`, which re-executes and prints the console log.

- We don't have to store the current time since we return a new value in every call to get().
- The other mysterious detail is when the atom becomes *unobserved*. This happens when we dispose of autorun() after three seconds, causing the onBecomeUnobserved callback to be invoked on the atom. Inside the callback, we stop the timer and clean up the resource.

Since Atoms are just the nodes of the dependency tree, we need a construct that can store the value of the observable. That is where the ObservableValue class comes in. Think of it as an Atom with value. MobX internally distinguishes between two kinds of observable values, ObservableValue and ComputedValue. Let's see them in turn.

ObservableValue

ObservableValue is a subclass of Atom that adds the ability to store the value of the observable. It also adds a few more capabilities such as providing hooks for intercepting a value change and observing the value. This is also part of the definition for ObservableValue. Here is a simplified definition of ObservableValue:

```
class ObservableValue extends Atom {
    value;

    get() {
        /* ... */
        this.reportObserved();
    }

    set(value) {
        /* Pass through interceptor, which may modify the value (newValue)
... */

        this.value = newValue;
        this.reportChanged();
    }

    intercept(handler) {}
    observe(listener, fireImmediately) {}
}
```

Notice the calls to reportObserved() in the get() method and reportChanged() in the set() method. These are the places where the atom's value is read and written to. By invoking these methods, an ObservableValue participates in the reactivity system. Also note that intercept() and observe() are not really part of the reactivity system. They are more like *event emitters* that hook into the changes happening to the observable value. These events are not affected by transactions, which means that they are not queued up till the end of the batch and instead fire immediately.

An ObservableValue is also the foundation for all of the higher-level constructs in MobX. This includes Boxed Observables, Observable Objects, Observable Arrays, and Observable Maps. The values stored in these data structures are instances of an ObservableValue.

The thinnest wrapper around an ObservableValue is the boxed observable, which you create using observable.box(). This API literally gives you back an instance of the ObservableValue. You can use this to call any of the methods on ObservableValue, as you can see in the following snippet:

```
import {observable} from 'mobx';

const count = observable.box(0);

count.intercept(change => {
    console.log('Intercepted:', change);

    return change; // No change
    // Prints
    // Intercepted: {object: ObservableValue$$1, type: "update", newValue:
1}
    // Intercepted: {object: ObservableValue$$1, type: "update", newValue:
2}
});

count.observe(change => {
    console.log('Observed:', change);
    // Prints
    // Observed: {object: ObservableValue$$1, type: "update", newValue: 1}
    // Observed: {object: ObservableValue$$1, type: "update", newValue: 2,
oldValue: 1}
});

// Increment
count.set(count.get() + 1);

count.set(count.get() + 1);
```

ComputedValue

The other kind of *observable value* that you can have in an observable tree is the
`ComputedValue`. This is different from an `ObservableValue` in many ways. An
`ObservableValue` provides storage for the underlying atom and has its *own value*. All the
data structures provided by MobX, such as Observable Object/Array/Map, rely on the
`ObservableValue` to store the leaf-level values. `ComputedValue` is special in the sense
that it does not have an intrinsic value of its own. Its *value*, as the name suggests, is
computed from other observables, including other computed values:

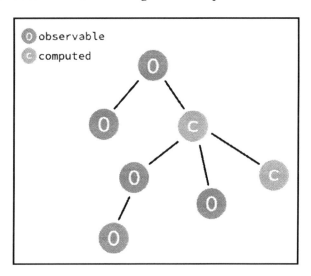

This becomes evident in the definition of `ComputedValue`, where it does not subclass `Atom`.
Instead, it has an interface that is similar to `ObservableValue`, except for the ability to
intercept. The following is a simplified definition that highlights the interesting parts:

```
class ComputedValue {
    get () {
        /* ... */
        reportObserved (this);
        /* ... */
    }

    set (value) { /* rarely applicable */ }

    observe (listener, fireImmediately) {}
}
```

An important thing to notice in the preceding snippet is that since a ComputedValue does not rely on an Atom, it uses a different approach for reportObserved(). This is a lower-level implementation that establishes a link between the observable and the observer. This is also used by Atom internally so that the behavior is exactly the same. Additionally, there is no call to reportChanged() as the setter for a ComputedValue is not well-defined.

As you can see, a ComputedValue is mostly a read-only observable. Although MobX provides a way to *set* a computed value, in most cases, it doesn't really make much sense. A setter for a computed value has to apply the reverse computation of the getter. This is almost impossible in most cases. Consider the example from earlier in this chapter about the description of a cart. This is a computed value that produces a string from other observables, like items and coupons. What would the *setter* for this computed property look like? It has to parse the string and somehow arrive at the values for items and coupons. That is definitely not possible. Thus, in general, it is better to treat ComputedValue as a readonly observable.

Since a computed value depends on other observables, the actual *value computation* is more like a side effect. It is a side effect of a change in any of the depending observables. MobX refers to this computation as a derivation. A derivation, as we will see a little later, is synonymous with reactions, emphasizing the side effect aspect of computation.

A ComputedValue is the only kind of node in the dependency tree that is an observable as well as an observer. Its value is an observable and due to its dependency on other observables, it is also an observer.

ObservableValue = Observable only
Reaction = Observer only
ComputedValue = Both observable and observer

Efficient computation

The derivation function of a ComputedValue could be an expensive operation. So, it is prudent to cache this value and compute as lazily as possible. That is the norm in MobX and it employs a bunch of optimizations to make this a lazy evaluation:

- To start with, a value is never computed unless explicitly requested or there is a reaction that depends on this ComputedValue. As expected, when there are no observers, it will not be computed at all.
- Once computed, its value is cached for future reads. It will stay that way until a depending observable signals a change (via its reportChanged()) and causes the derivation to re-evaluate.

- A `ComputedValue` can depend on other computed values creating a dependency tree. It does not recompute unless the immediate children have changed. If there is a change deep in the dependency tree, it waits until the immediate dependencies have changed. This behavior improves efficiency and does not recompute unnecessarily.

As you can see, there are multiple levels of optimization baked into a `ComputedValue`. It is highly recommended to leverage the power of computed properties to represent the various nuances of domain logic and its UI.

Derivation

So far, we have seen the building blocks of MobX, which represent the observable state with `Atoms`, `ObservableValue`, and `ComputedValue`. These are good to construct the reactive state graph of your application. But the true power of reactivity is unleashed with the use of derivations or reactions. Together, the observables and reactions form the yin-yang of MobX. Each relies on the other to fuel the reactive system.

A derivation or a reaction is where the tracking happens. It keeps track of all the observables used in the context of a derivation or reaction. MobX will listen to their `reportObserved()` and add them to the list of tracked observables (`ObservableValue` or `ComputedValue`). Any time the observable calls `reportChanged()` (which will happen when it's mutated), MobX will schedule a run of all the connected observers.

 We will be using *derivation* and *reaction* interchangeably. Both are intended to convey the execution of a side effect that uses the observables to produce a new value (*derivation*) or a side effect (*reaction*). The tracking behavior is common between these two types and hence we will use them synonymously.

The cycle of derivation

MobX uses a `globalState` to keep a reference to the currently executing *derivation* or *reaction*. Whenever a reaction is running, all observables that fire their `reportObserved()` will be tagged to this reaction. In fact, the relationship is bi-directional. An *observable* keeps track of all of its observers (reactions), while a *reaction* keeps track of all the observables it is currently observing. The currently executing reaction will be added as an *observer* for each of the observables. If the observer was already added, it will be ignored.

The observers all give back a disposer function when you set them up. We have already seen this with the return values of `autorun()`, `reaction()`, or `when()`, which are disposer functions. On calling this disposer, the observer will be removed from the connected observables:

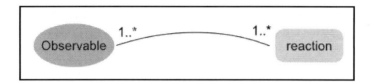

During the execution of a reaction, only the existing observables are considered for tracking. However, it is possible that in a different run of the same reaction, some new observables are referenced. This is possible when a piece of code executes that was originally skipped due to some branching logic. Since new observables can be discovered while tracking a reaction, MobX keeps a check on the observables. New ones are added to the list of observables, while ones that are not used anymore will be removed. Removal of an observable doesn't happen immediately; they are queued up for removal after completion of the current reaction.

In this interplay between observables and reactions, the **actions** seem to be missing sorely. Well, not entirely. They do have a role to play. As mentioned several times in this book, actions are the recommended way to mutate observables. An action creates a transaction boundary and ensures all change notifications are fired only after completion. These actions can also be nested, resulting in a nested transaction. It is only when the top most *action* (or transaction) completes that the notifications will be fired. This also means that none of the *reactions* run while a transaction (nested or not) is in progress. MobX treats this transaction boundary as a **batch** and keeps track of the nesting internally. During a batch, all reactions will be queued up and executed at the end of the top-most batch.

When the queued up reactions execute, the cycle begins yet again. It will track observables, link them with the executing derivation, add any newly discovered observables, and queue up any reactions that are found during a batch. If there are no more batches, MobX deems itself to be stable and goes back to waiting for any observable mutations.

An interesting thing about reactions is that they could re-trigger themselves. Inside a reaction, you can read an observable and also fire an action that mutates that same *observable*. This may happen within the same block of code or indirectly via some function invoked from the reaction. The only requirement is that it should *not* lead to an infinite loop. MobX expects the reaction to become stable as quickly as possible.

If, for some reason, it takes more than **100** iterations and there is no stability, MobX will bail out with an exception.

Reaction doesn't converge to a stable state after 100 iterations. There is probably a cycle in the reactive function: `Reaction[Reaction@14]`

Without the upper limit of 100 iterations, it would cause a stack overflow at runtime, making it much harder to track down its cause. MobX protects you from this predicament by guarding with the **100-iterations** limit. Note that it does not forbid you from cyclic dependencies but assists in identifying the code that is causing the instability (infinite loop).

A simple snippet that is unstable even after *100 iterations of the reaction* is shown as follows. This reaction observes the `counter` observable, and also modifies it by invoking the `spinLoop()` action. This causes the reaction to run again and again until it gives up after *100 iterations*:

```
class Infinite {
    @observable counter = 0;

    constructor() {
        reaction(
            () => this.counter,
            counterValue => {
                console.log(`Counter is ${counterValue}`);
                this.spinLoop();
            },
        );
    }

    @action
    spinLoop() {
        this.counter = this.counter + 1;
    }
}

new Infinite().spinLoop();
```

```
/* Console log:
Reaction doesn't converge to a stable state after 100 iterations. Probably
there is a cycle in the reactive function: Reaction[Reaction@14]
*/
```

As you can tell, executing a derivation or reaction is crucial for establishing the link between *observables* and *observers*. Without a *reaction*, there is no life in the reactivity system. It would just be a collection of observables. You could still fire actions and mutate them, but it would still be very static and non-reactive. Reactions (Derivations) complete the triad of *Observables-Actions-Reactions* and pump life into this reactive system.

Ultimately, **reactions** are the ones that *pull values* from your state and fire up the whole reactive process!

Exception handling

Handling errors is considered an essential part of MobX reactions. In fact, it provides an option to supply an error handler (onError) for autorun(), reaction(), and when(), and in the case of computed(), it will throw the error back to you any time the computed value is read. In each of these cases, MobX continues to work as expected.

Internally, MobX puts additional try-catch blocks around the execution of reactions and derivations. It will catch the errors thrown inside these blocks and propagate them back to you via the onError handlers or when a computed value is read. This behavior ensures that you can continue running your reactions and take any recovery measures inside the onError handlers.

If there is no onError handler specified for a reaction, MobX also has a global onReactionError() handler that will be called for any exception thrown in a reaction. You can register a listener for these global reaction errors to do things like error monitoring, reporting, and so on:

```
onReactionError(handler-function: (error, reaction) => { })
```

handler-function: A function accepting the error and the instance of a reaction as its arguments.

Before a global `onReactionError` handler is called, MobX first checks for an `onError` handler for the reaction that is failing. It's only when that doesn't exist that the global handler is invoked.

Now, if for some reason you don't want this behavior where MobX catches the exception and reports it on a global `onReactionError` handler, you have a way out. By configuring MobX with `configure({ disableErrorBoundaries: true })`, you will get a regular exception thrown at the *point of failure*. You will now be expected to handle it via a *try-catch* block right inside the reaction.

`configure({ disableErrorBoundaries: true })` shouldn't be used in normal circumstances as leaving exceptions unchecked can corrupt the internal state of MobX. However, turning on this configuration can help you in debugging since it will make the exception uncaught. You can now pause your debugger on the exact statement that causes the exception.

The API layer

This is the consumer facing, outermost layer of MobX and builds on the foundations mentioned thus far. The prominent APIs that stand out in this layer include the ones seen throughout this book: `observable()`, `observable.box()`, `computed()`, `extendObservable()`, `action()`, `reaction()`, `autorun()`, `when()`, and others. Of course, we also have the decorators, such as `observable.ref`, `observable.deep`, `observable.shallow`, `action.bound`, `computed.struct`, and so on.

The core data structures such as `ObservableObject`, `ObservableArray`, and `ObservableMap` rely on the `ObservableValue` to store all of their values.

For an `ObservableObject`...:

- A key-value pair has its value backed by an `ObservableValue`.
- Every computed property, as expected, is backed by a `ComputedValue`.
- The `keys()` method of an *ObservableObject* is also backed by an `Atom`. This is needed as you may be iterating on the `keys()` in one of your reactions. When a key gets added or removed, you want your reactions to execute again. This atom for `keys()` fires the `reportChanged()` for additions and removals and ensures that the connected reactions are re-executed.

For an `ObservableArray`...:

- Every indexed value is backed by `ObservableValue`.
- The `length` property is explicitly backed by an `Atom`. Note that *ObservableArray* has the same interface as JavaScript arrays. In **MobX 4**, it was an array-like data structure, which has become a real JS Array in **MobX 5** (backed by an ES6 *Proxy*). The reads and writes on `length` will result in `reportObserved()` and `reportChanged()` being called on the atom. In fact, when any of the methods like *map, reduce, filter*, and so on are used, the backing `Atom` is used to fire `reportObserved()`. For any mutating methods like *splice, push, pop, shift*, and so on, the `reportChanged()` is fired. This ensures the connected reactions fire as expected.

For an `ObservableMap`...:

- A *key-value* pair has its value backed by an `ObservableValue`.
- Just like *ObservableObject*, it too maintains an instance of `Atom` for the `keys()` method. Any addition or removal of keys is notified with a `reportChanged()` on the atom. Calling the `keys()` method itself will fire the `reportObserved()` on the atom.

The collections in MobX, which are objects, arrays, and maps, are essentially collections of observable boxes (`ObservableValue`). They may be organized as a list or as a map, or combined to create complex structures.

All of these data structures also expose the `intercept()` and `observe()` methods that allows granular interception and observation of values. By building on the foundations of `Atom`, `ObservableValue`, and *derivations*, MobX gives you a powerful toolbox of APIs to build sophisticated state management solutions in your applications.

Transparent functional reactive programming

MobX is considered a **Transparent functional reactive programming (TFRP)** system. Yes, too many adjectives in that line! Let's break it down word by word.

It is Transparent...

Connecting the *observables* to the *observers*, it allows the observers to react to changes in observables. This is a basic expectation we have from MobX and the way we establish these connections feels very intuitive. There is no explicit wiring besides the use of decorators and dereferencing observables inside the observer. Because of the low overhead in wiring, MobX becomes very *declarative*, where you express your intent without worrying about the machinery. The automatic connections established between the *observables* and *observers* enables the *reactive system* to function autonomously. This makes MobX a *transparent* system as the work of connecting observables with observers is essentially lifted away. The usage of an observable inside a reaction is enough to wire the two.

It is reactive...

This reactivity is also very fine-grained. The dependency tree of observables can be as simple as you need and also equally as deep. The interesting part is that you never worry about the complexity of wiring or the efficiency. MobX has a deep knowledge of your dependencies and ensures the efficiencies by reacting only when needed. There is no polling or excessive events being fired as the dependencies keep changing. Thus, MobX is also a very reactive system.

It is functional...

Functional programming, as we know, is about leveraging the power of functions to perform data flow transformations. By using a variety of functional operators like map, reduce, filter, compose, and so on, we can apply transformations on *input data* and produce output values. The catch in the case of MobX is that the *input data* is an observable, a time *varying* value. MobX combines the qualities of a reactive system and ensures the functional -transformations are automatically applied when the input data (observable) changes. It does this in a transparent fashion, as discussed earlier, by establishing implicit connections between the observables and reactions.

This combination of qualities makes MobX a TFRP system.

 From the author's point of view, the *origins* of the acronymn TFRP has come from the following article: `https://github.com/meteor/docs/blob/version-NEXT/long-form/tracker-manual.md`.

Value Oriented Programming

MobX is also about **Value Oriented Programming (VOP)**, where you focus on the change in values, its dependencies, and its propagation across the reactive system. With VOP, you focus on *What are the connected values?* rather than the *How are the values connected?* Its counterpart is **Event Oriented Programming (EOP)**, where you focus on a stream of events to notify changes. Events only report what has happened with no notion of dependencies. It's at a lower level conceptually, compared to Value-Oriented-Programming.

VOP relies on events to do its job internally. When a value changes, events are raised to notify the change. The handlers for these events will then propagate the value to all listeners (*observers*) of that *observable value*. This usually results in a reaction/derivation being invoked. Thus, reactions and derivations, which are the side effects of the value change, are at the tail-end of the value propagation event.

Thinking in VOP raises the level of abstraction, bringing you closer to the domain that you are dealing with. Rather than worrying about the mechanism of value propagation, you just focus on establishing connections via observables, computed properties, and observers (reactions/derivations). This, as we know, is the triad of MobX: *Observables-Actions-Reactions*. This style of thinking is very ***declarative*** in nature: the *What versus How* of value changes. As you get more steeped into this mindset, many of the scenarios in state management become much more tenable. You will be amazed at the *simplicity, power, and efficiency* that this paradigm offers.

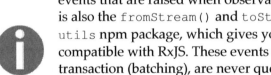

If you do need to dive deeper into the eventing layer, MobX has the `intercept()` and `observe()` APIs. They allow you to hook into the events that are raised when observables are *added, updated, or deleted*. There is also the `fromStream()` and `toStream()` APIs from the `mobx-utils` npm package, which gives you a stream of events that are compatible with RxJS. These events don't participate in the MobX transaction (batching), are never queued up, and always fire immediately.

It is rare to use the eventing APIs in consumer code; they are mostly used by tools and utility functions such as `spy()`, `trace()`, and so on to give insight into the event layer of MobX.

Summary

With this under-the-hood peek at MobX, you can appreciate the power of the TFRP system, exposed with a surprisingly simple API. The layers of functionality, starting with the `Atoms`, wrapped by `ObservableValue`, with APIs and higher-level data structures, offer a comprehensive solution to model your domains.

Internally, MobX manages all the connections between the observables and observers (reactions/derivations). It is done automatically with minimal interference to your usual style of programming. As a developer, you write code that feels natural, with MobX lifting away the complexity of managing the reactive connections.

MobX is an open source project that has been battle-tested for various domains, accepted contributions from developers all over the world, and has been constantly maturing over the years. With this inside look at MobX, we sure hope to reduce the barriers to contributing to this powerful state management library.

Other Books You May Enjoy

If you enjoyed this book, you may be interested in these other books by Packt:

Vuex Quick Start Guide
Andrea Koutifaris

ISBN: 978-1-78899-993-9

- Moving from classical MVC to a Flux-like architecture
- Implementing predictable centralized state management in your applications using Vuex
- Using ECMAScript 6 features for developing a real application
- Using webpack in conjunction with Vue single file components
- Testing your Vue/Vuex applications using Karma/Jasmine and inject-loader
- Simple and effective Test Driven Development
- Extending your application with Vuex plugins

Learning Redux
Daniel Bugl

ISBN: 978-1-78646-239-8

- Understand why and how Redux works
- Implement the basic elements of Redux
- Use Redux in combination with React/Angular to develop a web application
- Debug a Redux application
- Interface with external APIs with Redux
- Implement user authentication with Redux
- Write tests for all elements of a Redux application
- Implement simple and more advanced routing with Redux
- Learn about server-side rendering with Redux and React
- Create higher-order reducers for Redux
- Extend the Redux store via middleware

Leave a review - let other readers know what you think

Please share your thoughts on this book with others by leaving a review on the site that you bought it from. If you purchased the book from Amazon, please leave us an honest review on this book's Amazon page. This is vital so that other potential readers can see and use your unbiased opinion to make purchasing decisions, we can understand what our customers think about our products, and our authors can see your feedback on the title that they have worked with Packt to create. It will only take a few minutes of your time, but is valuable to other potential customers, our authors, and Packt. Thank you!

Index

Printed in Poland
by Amazon Fulfillment
Poland Sp. z o.o., Wrocław

25095093R00134